ARE YOU A MAN OR A WOMAN IN THE MINISTRY? ARE YOU MARRIED TO SOMEONE CHOSEN BY GOD?

You Are Highly Favored!!!

JUDITH HARRELL

WESTBOW
PRESS®
A DIVISION OF THOMAS NELSON
& ZONDERVAN

WestBow Press books may be ordered through booksellers or by contacting:

WestBow Press
A Division of Thomas Nelson & Zondervan
1663 Liberty Drive
Bloomington, IN 47403
www.westbowpress.com
844-714-3454

Scripture taken from the King James Version of the Bible.

If you would like Elect Lady Judith A. Harrell, Author of this
book to speak at one of you events, please Email to:
GR8ERMNISTRY@VERIZON.NET

ISBN: 978-1-6642-5880-8 (sc)
ISBN: 978-1-6642-5879-2 (e)

Print information available on the last page.

WestBow Press rev. date: 03/22/2022

THIS IS GOD'S GUIDE TO ENJOY BEING MARRIED

AND ESPECIALLY TO A MAN OR
WOMEN IN THE MINISTRY.

I would like to dedicate this book to my awesome husband, Bishop John S. Harrell who has treated me like a Queen for forty-seven years. He has treated my daughter like a Princess for thirty-six years. He has loved, cherished, nurtured, prayed, fasted, and counseled me with divine love. I have learned so much by his Godly example. He has used wisdom and knowledge from the Lord, and a multitude of patience with me until I have become, "The Greatest Woman he has ever met", as he stated.

I would like to dedicate this book to my daughter (Shekinah M. Harrell) for encouraging me to write this book for about twenty years or more. Thank you again Shekinah, I would have never copyrighted or published this book without your constant encouragement.

I would like to thank all of God's Prophets and Prophetesses that sent me the Word from God to write this book numerous times.

Also, I would like to dedicate this book in the memory of my oldest sister Elect Lady Vurnadette C. Hill who was a Pastor's wife that has inspired me all of my life concerning being married to a man in ministry.

CONTENTS

Introduction xi

Chapter 1   You are Highly Favored 1
Chapter 2   The Meaning of a Holy and Happy Marriage 9
Chapter 3   A Message to All Wives 17
Chapter 4   A Bishop's Wife's Qualifications 19
Chapter 5   A Deacon's Wives Qualifications 37
Chapter 6   An Elders's Wife and All Other Clergy Wives 43
Chapter 7   Virtous Women 45
Chapter 8   The Things My First Pastor Taught Me,
             (How To Be A Good Saved Wife) 49
Chapter 9   Aged Women Teach All Women
             Especially the Young Women 51
Chapter 10   How Thou Ought to Behave Thyself in
             the House of God. 57
Chapter 11   (I Corinthians 13, Kjv)-The Love Chapter 67
Chapter 12   Husbands (God's Rule For You By Scriptures). 73
Chapter 13   (From the Wife's Perspective) Reasons
             Why I Believe I've Been Happily Married 103
Chapter 14   (Husband's Perspective) Reasons Why
             My Husband is Happily Married. 109
Chapter 15   Husbands/ Happy 47Th Anniversary 111
Chapter 16   I Have Gotten A Man From the Lord!!!!! 117
Chapter 17   A letter to my Husband for his Birthday 121
Chapter 18   A Letter to My Husband on Father's Day 125
Last Chapter Only for Women that Marry Holy Men and are
             Very Serious About Pleasing God. 129

About the Author...151

INTRODUCTION

You may be troubled at this saying that you are an Apostle's wife, Presiding Bishop's wife, Bishop's wife, a Pastor's wife, a Prophet's wife, an Elder's wife, an Evangelist's wife, a Minister's wife, or a Deacon's wife like Mary was troubled. However, fear not, for thou hast found favor with God. The Lord is with thee and you are blessed among women.

You are always under the telescope by the Church World and you may be troubled in your spirit and feeling pressured to be the PERFECT WOMAN OF GOD THAT IS MARRIED TO A MAN IN MINISTRY. You wonder, is it possible to live a normal, happy, peaceful, married life living with A MAN OF GOD in a day like this?

Absolutely! LET ME TAKE THE WEIGHT OFF YOUR SHOULDERS by reading this book.

In this book I have Bible Scriptures and forty-seven years of experience of being married to a Man of God that was elevated from a Minister, Elder, Pastor, Bishop, and presently a Pastor and a Presiding Bishop over a church organization.

ONE

You are Highly Favored

TO
APOSTLE'S, A PRESIDING BISHOP'S,
A PASTOR'S, PROPHET'S,
ELDER'S, MINISTER'S, EVANGELIST'S,
OR DEACON'S WIVES?
ARE YOU MARRIED
TO A MAN OR WOMAN IN THE MINISTRY???
YOU ARE HIGHLY FAVORED!!!

AND THE ANGEL CAME IN UNTO HER, AND SAID,
"HAIL, THOU THAT ART HIGHLY FAVOURED,
THE LORD IS WITH THEE: BLESSED ART
THOU AMONG WOMEN" (LUKE 1:28, KJV).

YOU ARE HIGHLY FAVORED BY GOD AND
THE LORD IS WITH THEE, AND YOU ALSO
ARE BLESSED AMONG WOMEN.

WEBSTER DEFINES **FAVOR** AS GOOD WILL, KIND REGARD, KINDNESS, SUPPORT, DISPOSITION TO AID, BEFRIEND, PROMOTE. A KIND ACT OR OFFICE; KINDNESS DONE OR GRANTED; BENEVOLENCE SHOWN BY WORD OR DEED; ANY ACT OF GRACE OR GOOD WILL, TO WISH SUCCESS TO; TO ENCOURAGE; A GIFT, PRESENT, OR A TOKEN OF LOVE.

YOU ARE A GIFT AND A PRESENT; YOU ARE BESTOWED TO YOUR HUSBAND AND THE PEOPLE OF GOD AS AN

EVIDENCE OF GOOD WILL, A TOKEN OF LOVE. YOU
ARE AN ADVANTAGE, TO HELP TO SUCCEED, TO MAKE
POSSIBLE OR EASY, TO TREAT GENTLY OR CAREFULLY.
YOU ARE TO REGARD WITH KINDNESS, TO SUPPORT,
TO AID, OR HAVE THE DISPOSITION TO AID, TO WISH
SUCCESS TO, TO BEFRIEND, AND TO ENCOURAGE YOUR
HUSBAND AND THE PEOPLE IN THE LORD'S KINGDOM.

**You are not like other women and we can not be like other
women.** The Lord had a divine purpose for us to live with Holy
Ghost filled men that are leaders and preachers of the Gospel of
Jesus Christ. Our Savior chose Mary to carry the Holy Ghost and
**he chose us to live with the Holy Ghost and support a Great Man
of God!** You must understand that our risen King **chose us just as
he chose our husbands.** It does not matter how you were raised or
how you feel about yourself, God handpicked us from the beginning
of time to be in the office of a wife to a man in ministry. It is an
office (**Webster** states an office is a special duty or something done
for another). God chose us for a special duty and that duty is to live
with a Holy man of God. Also, a wife is a job; (**Webster** says a job is
a special duty or function). You have the second highest job, a special
duty, and a function in the kingdom of God. Your assignment
was first given to you by God and you are to **support, aid,** and
encourage your husband to be successful! **Webster** also states
a job is a position at which one regularly works for pay, however,
your pay will come directly from Heaven. You have a career (a
profession followed as a permanent occupation). **Your career, your
profession,** and **your permanent occupation** is to be **a wife to this
awesome Man of God.** Your **career is a lifelong career** that **will
not end until you die. It is your destiny!** You can not run from
your calling** or take this **calling lightly.** It is a high calling that is
serious, honest, and **honorable!** You have been **called, summoned,**
and **ordered** by Our King of Kings **to be a wife to the Man of God.**

Mary was approximately between twelve or sixteen years old and was chosen to give birth to Jesus Christ. It was a disgrace for someone so young to conceive a child without being married. It was a greater shame or disgrace in Bible days to be found with child without a husband. However, the angel said "thou shalt conceive in thy womb, bring forth a son, and shalt call his name Jesus". We have been **chosen, highly favored**, and **the Lord is with us**. We are blessed among women to carry and live with a Holy Ghost filled Man! We are there to help bring forth the assignment of a husband which shall be called an Apostle, a Presiding Bishop, a Bishop, a Pastor, a Prophet, an Elder, a Minister, an Evangelist, or a Deacon.

The angel told Mary that "He shall be great, and shall be called the Son of the Highest: and the Lord God shall give unto him the throne of His father David: And He shall reign over the house of Jacob forever; and of his kingdom there shall be no end" **(Luke 1:32 & 33 KJV).**

I'm telling you that you must first believe in your husband that he is Great. If you do not think he is great no one else will believe he is Great. "How beautiful are the feet of them that preach the gospel of peace, and bring glad tidings of good things!" **(Romans 10:15, KJV).** Your husband is Great because of the Holy Ghost, his anointing, and the calling God has put on his life. He is not an ordinary man; he is a Man of God that has been chosen to oversee a ministry or assist with the Kingdom of God; there is no end to serving in ministry! Come to the realization that you can not be inconsistent or unstable. You must always remember that you have to be committed to the work of the Lord just like your husband. As a wife, you must always believe in your husband's ministry and **you must not do anything to hurt or harm the ministry.** Your spouse belongs to God and the ministry. He has to put the Lord **first** and **you second**; however, when you grow in your office together, the both of you will **put the work of the ministry first!**

Then said Mary unto the angel, "How shall this be, seeing I know not a man?" **(Luke 1:34, KJV).** You may be wondering in your mind how shall this be also? How can I hold this precious office as the wife to a great Man of God? No matter what your age, you may feel inexperienced, and feel that you can not perform in this office, but Mary did not feel qualified either. **First**, you must understand that **(I Corinthians 1:25 & 27 & 28, KJV)** states "Because the foolishness of God is wiser than men; and the weakness of God is stronger than men. But God has chosen the foolish things of the world to confound the wise; and God hath chosen the weak things of the world to confound the things which are mighty; And base things of the world, and things which are despised, hath God chosen, yea, and things which are not, to bring to nought things that are:" **Secondly**, you must have the understanding that you did not stumble into this position. It was not an accident. The Lord has been preparing you for this job all your life. Our Savior chose you and told you that you are highly favored, the Lord is with thee, and you are blessed among women. God knows what He is doing and you must believe that. If you could not do the job, he would have never called you. The Most High does not give you a job you can not do.

And the angel answered and said unto her, "The Holy Ghost shall come upon thee, and the power of the Highest shall overshadow thee: therefore, also that holy thing which shall be born of thee shall be called the Son of God" **(Luke 1:35, KJV).**

This is the part of the answer how shall this be? **Thirdly**, the Holy Ghost shall come upon thee, and the power of the Highest shall overshadow thee. You must have the Holy Ghost with power. You must continue to fast, pray, and allow the Holy Ghost to overshadow thee in this precious office as the wife to Great Holy Men. "You must be fervent in the Spirit" **(Romans 12:11, KJV).**

I am repeating these statements intentionally because I want you to get this in your mind, heart, spirit, and soul. We are wives of Great Men of God and we are highly favored. We are very fortunate that Our Savior called us to be in this position. The Lord is with us and He will never leave us as we serve in this ministry. **Be strong and of a good courage, fear not, nor be afraid of them: for the LORD thy God, he it is that doth go with thee; he will not fail thee, nor forsake thee). (Deuteronomy 31:6, KJV)** Be strong and of good courage, fear not the position God has given you as this man's wife. Do not be afraid of Church People, your husband's members that he oversees or members of other churches. The Lord thy God, gave you this position and He promised to go with you. Our Lord will not fail you or forsake you in this position, at home, or in church. We are truly blessed among women to be called by God into this office. **<u>Fear not, for thou hast found favor with God.</u>**

Society may cause you to perceive your duty as a mere house wife. The devil wants to have a field day in your mind, making you feel like you are wasting your time, energy, effort, and life just sitting at home being a house wife. God help you if the kids are gone and you are going through "empty nest syndrome". Woe is me! You feel like a big fat zero. The devil is a Big Fat Liar! You are not just a house wife! You hold the most important job, position, profession, career, and permanent occupation in the world. Your position is the second most important office next to your husband in the church. You hold the office of a wife to a Man in the ministry. And the Lord God said, "It is not good that the man should be alone; I will make him a help meet for him" **(Genesis 2:18, KJV).** God knew the importance of a woman in a man's life since the beginning of time. **<u>It is vital that a man</u>** and **<u>especially a man of God not to be alone</u>. <u>He needs his rib</u>, <u>his help meet</u>, <u>his aid</u>, <u>his support</u>, <u>his gift from God</u>, <u>his present</u>, <u>his token of love</u>, <u>his advantage</u>, <u>his evidence of good will</u>, <u>his act of kindness</u>,** and **<u>his act of grace</u>;** yes, I am talking about you! Woman of God! The Men need us more than you will ever know! Sometimes it takes a man years to express how **necessary, vital,** and **important you are to be his wife.** Just hold on and believe what I say. You are the most important person in his life and to the ministry.

You are more important than the President's wife of the United States. You have not seen a President run for office without a wife. Your position is very important and you have to be careful how you conduct yourself. God and the world are looking at you. Many are going to try to find fault in the wife of a Man in ministry. Fear not because you are highly favored, very fortunate, the Lord is with you, and you are blessed among women. "Fear not, Mary: for thou hast found favour with God" **(Luke 1:30, KJV).** "For with God nothing shall be impossible" **(Luke 1:37, KJV).**

"And Mary said, Behold the handmaid of the Lord; be it unto me according to thy word" **(Luke 1:38, KJV).** After hearing what the angel said, she was **willing to accept her office and be glad about it.** The devil is going to try to continue to fight us with the idea that we are not important; we are useless, irrelevant, especially if you are not working and not contributing finances to your household. However, the devil is a liar! I hope you will ponder all the words that I have said during this book to resist the devil! Fight him when he comes in your mind to attack you with this negative thought that you are not worth anything! **We are priceless**! Tell the devil that God made me highly favored, the Lord is with me, and I am blessed among women because I am the wife of a Man of God! Our Savior found favor with me and made me a wife of a Man in Ministry!

I had a goal in life to remain single until I got a doctor's degree, achieved a GS-13 government position, travel the world and visualized myself as a successful business woman. I never reached that goal, I had to submit to God's plan for my life and you must have peace with what God has ordained for your life. I'm not saying you have to give up your dreams but this was God's plan for me. Do not sit home another day fighting with God or yourself. "Submit means to accept or yield to a superior force or to the authority or will of another person. Submit yourselves therefore to God. Resist the devil, and he will flee from you" **(James 4:7, KJV).** Obedience is better than sacrifice **(I Samuel 15:22, KJV).** "If ye be willing and obedient, ye shall eat the good of the land: But if ye refuse and rebel, ye shall be devoured (destroyed) with the sword: for the mouth of the Lord hath spoken it" **(Isaiah 1:19 &20, KJV).** The Lord wants to use you as a Godly woman living with a great man in ministry! Your office is the wife of a man with an assignment. This is **your mission in life**; **your purpose** and **who you are**! The wife of a man of God **is your calling**! **You have been summoned** and **ordained** by God. This is **your job**, **career**, **profession**, and **your permanent occupation**. Even after the children leave home, you still have a calling by God and you must **be faithful until death.** You are the spouse of a man of God! **Fast** and **pray** until your heart, soul, mind, and spirit say unto **God, "nevertheless not as I will, but as thou wilt"** as stated in **(Matthew 26:39, KJV).** It is his will that you be the wife of a man of God; be happy and do not worry. **(I Timothy 6:6, KJV)** states, "But Godliness with contentment is great gain". **Embrace it, cherish it, know it, and ponder it in your heart** that **I am chosen by God and highly favored, very fortunate to be the wife of a man of God.** The Lord is with me every step of the journey and I am blessed among women because I was called and chosen by God to be the wife of a Godly man. **"I must work the work of him that sent me, while it is day: the night cometh, when no man can work"** **(John 9:4, KJV).**

TWO

THE MEANING OF A HOLY
AND HAPPY MARRIAGE

You are Chosen by God, and Highly Favored and very fortunate to be the wife of a Man in ministry. You are Chosen and Highly Favored you already know what a Holy Marriage is. Marriage is a legally recognized union between a man and a woman to make them one physically, mentally, and spiritually. This book is especially talking about a legally union between a man and woman that's Holy Ghost filled.

Marriage is a covenant, agreement, and a commitment to live together the rest of your lives. In a Christian marriage vows are made before God to bear with each other regardless of the circumstances. It is to supply each other's needs for mutual fulfillment, partnership, respect, and understanding. The Lord holds marriage in high esteem because it is a model of the church. When God took a rib from Adam, this exemplifies the church that came out of the side of Jesus when He died on the cross; out of his side came blood and water **(John 19:34, Acts 20:28, KJV).** The Lord ordained marriage in the Garden of Eden.

(Genesis 2:18, KJV)

[18] And the LORD God said, it is not good that the man should be alone; I will make him an **help meet for him.**

(Genesis 2:24, KJV)

[24] Therefore shall a man leave his father and his mother, and shall **cleave unto his wife**: and they shall be **one flesh**.

It is not good that any man should be single, but have a help meet, a wife for him. Adam and Eve gave all marriages an example of cleaving to your wife and sticking to your husband. When God blessed Adam and Eve in the Garden of Eden they stayed together, and when God was displeased with them, they both were thrown out of the Garden of Eden and Adam and Eve remained united. In good times and bad times, you can still stay together and be happy.

A Holy Man has a natural need to protect and provide leadership for his wife and to be accepted by his wife. God made a Holy woman's desire, impulse, and aspiration to please her husband with a need to be protected and loved. Our Savior provides the fulfillment of these needs in the marriage. Both husband and wife enter in a relationship to esteem, admire, to be fair, and be honest with one another. In a Holy Marriage you must trust each other 100%. Trust in a marriage is a BIG DEAL. Many times, our own insecurities cause us to mistrust our mates. If we feel good about ourselves, we can trust our mates. Remember we are saved and we should never do anything to cause our mates to loss trust. Resist the Devil and rebuke him with any thoughts of mistrust. You are both filled with the Holy Ghost so trust one another and each other. You both are saved and have nothing to hide.

Therefore, Women and Men of God should always be truthful about ourselves, let each other know where you are going at all times. Yes, you both are grown, but this is how you must show respect to each other.

Problems may and will arise in your marriage, but the Bible teaches us how to solve them all. Communication is vital in a Holy Marriage. Husbands and wives must always disclose, inform, relate, and reveal all problems by communication! Lack of communication in a marriage can cause trouble. If two people are in a house and do not communicate that is not a marriage that's just two people living under the same roof. Regardless how upset or angry you get, go sit down somewhere and calm down. Then come together and communicate together to solve the problem. It should be a discussion, not a screaming match!

(Hebrew 13:16, KJV)

[16] But to do good and to communicate forget not: for with such sacrifices God is well pleased.

You will always have a Happy Marriage when you learn to do good to each other and communicate about everything. God is well pleased when you learn the art of communicating like two saved people to resolve a problem. When your communication line is flowing, the both of you will love talking to each other. It will become a joy to sit and talk together because you will get to know each other better and become more than a married couple, but become the very best of friends.

Holy Woman of God you know that the lack of money can cause problems in the marriage. Sometimes you were accustomed to buying every new dress, shoes, and outfit when you were single. At times we spend more than we have or get our priorities mixed up. Never the less, Holy Woman of God your money is no longer your own. Holy Man of God your money is no longer just yours. Both of your finances belong to the marriage. It is no more my money, my car, my house or my apartment, "it is ours, we, and us." You are a business and you have meetings to control your business finances. You must teach each other to put priorities first, your tithes, church offerings, mortgage or rent, monthly expenses, and have an emergency savings. You must sit down and have a Home Budget. Resist the devil when you want to be selfish with your money and use it unwisely. Everything you do with your money affects the whole marriage. Husband and wife must come and reason with each other about money. **(ISAIAH 1:18, KJV)**

(Isaiah 1:18, KJV)

18 Come now, and **let us reason together**, saith the LORD: though your sins be as scarlet, they shall be as white as snow; though they be red like crimson, they shall be as wool.

If one or the both of you have a splurging and spending money problem, you should acknowledge it. Find out what the cause is because it could destroy a marriage. You do not get into financial problems only because of lack of money. People fall into money issues because of shortsightedness, wrong values, impulse control disorders, keeping up with the Jones, and measuring their self-worth by what they have instead of who they are. You will continue the cycle of paying off bills and then making new ones consistently unless you examine the emotional reasons behind your spending. Come together in fasting, praying, reading the Word of God, and possibly get professional help to conquer this problem. We are more than conquerors; we have the Almighty to help us.

(John 16:33, KJV) "Ye are of God, little children, and have overcome them: because greater is he that is in you, **than** he that is in the world."

(1 John 4:4, KJV) "Nay, in all these things **we are more than conquerors** through him that loved us."

Husbands and wives were both single at one time. They must learn that they are married now and old ways must change! From a single life to a married life style. Therefore, they **must seek God not to be** **self-centered**, **selfish**, or **lack patience**. They must not have uncontrollable tempers and not be demanding. Please make common sense and sound judgment when it comes to your marriage and business affairs. Do not be destructive, careless, insensitive or let people outside your marriage control your home. Do not speak about how your mother and father ran their marriage. Do not to be secretive, neither one of you should have any secrets now. Wives must learn to grow up. We can not be acting like little children, helpless, and weeping. I had just turned nineteen when I got married. My husband had to have a lot of patience with me, prayed and fasted. God revealed to him what I needed to grow up in the most beautiful way.

DO NOT BLAME ONE ANOTHER FOR THINGS THAT GO WRONG IN THE MARRIAGE:

During our marriage terrible things have happened to us. We had a fire in our apartment, everything we owned was burned up, and many other unfortunate things happened. We lost so many valuables. One thing we did not lose was our love for one another, it grew deeper and stronger. Trouble and difficult times make you see how deeply you really love each other. I told my husband if he goes down, he will not go down by himself, I will be right beside him. When he rises again, which he will, I still will be standing right beside him.

Holy Woman of God and Holy Man of God, the biggest misperception in marriage is the idea that if you love each other deeply, you shouldn't have to work at it. You do not know anyone until you say, "I do" and live with them. Loving someone in marriage, it means I am willing to invest the time, energy, and effort to make our love grow and marriage work no matter what. When two lives merge together, with one or two sets of finances, two sets of families, two sets of values, you must determine in both of your hearts, we are going to become one in spite of all these differences. In your first year of marriage it may be challenging, you did not pick the wrong person. Don't even think about leaving. You are just getting to know one another. Just keep working on it! You will learn each other's likes and dislikes and make your own rules for your marriage. You both have to put strong effort into finding common ground. After you marry you must love even harder than when you were dating.

My first year of marriage was a trail because I was spoiled, wanted my way, and I cried a lot to get my way. My husband was so patient, sweet, kind, compassionate, understanding and he allowed God to mold me into a beautiful wife. With his prayer and sweet guidance, God helped me grow up.

Also, my husband started his own church from scratch, a small broken-down Store Front with one door, no windows, and two members. I hated being a Pastor's Wife at nineteen years old because majority of the time my husband focused on God and the Church. Often young pastors get so zealous with God and His work they neglect time with their wife. At the age of nineteen it was very difficult to deal with so many situations and different kinds of people that were in the Church World. You will soon find out that every one that attend Church is not sweetly saved or even saved. One Sunday, I got my purse and said, "I am leaving this broken-down Church and my husband" I did not sign up for this. **For the first time in my life, a voice from Heaven said out loud from Heaven and told me, "If you leave him, I will kill you". It scared me so bad, I knew it was the voice of God.** I turned around and sit down in Church and my husband did not have no more trouble with me.

God spoke this to me because I could not see the **FUTURE**. God knew that he was going to be the center of our marriage and he was going help us to straighten everything out. He knew that we as a marriage couple would blossom into the greatest love story on the planet Earth. Our Love for each other was going to be Special, ordained by God, and an everlasting Love. God also knew we were going to be "THE GREATEST EXAMPLES OF A HAPPILY MARRIED COUPLE IN THE WORLD". God also knew that we were going to do Great things for the Kingdom as a Happily Married Couple and a Spiritual Team.

Therefore, God sent an older prophet to tell my husband Love God first, then put your wife second. Also, Our Savior spoke from Heaven to my Husband and told him Love me first, but Love your wife second, and then the Church. My young husband, twenty-three years old which was a Pastor became a new man! After God spoke to the both of us, our marriage began to be a beautiful Love Affair. Forty-seven years of marriage, we both love each other more deeply than when we said, "I do". I feel our love is so deep that we breath from the same lung, think from the same brain, and our hearts beat from the same heart.

The Almighty has blessed our marriage because we wanted it to work and God ordained for us to be married before the foundation of the World! However, we worked together to make our union work. As I matured, we started a wonderful procedure. We would say, "What can I do to make our marriage better? Then each one of us would do that, whether it was small, simple, or challenging. We must share one another's passions, support their best interest, be supportive to the things that are important to one another. Always let your husband and wife know that you love them and are proud of each other.

Sometimes you may feel that you are giving more than what is reciprocated, but if you are committed, you will continue to give.

Don't think so much about how much you are giving, but your reward in the end. Don't wait for your partner to meet you halfway. Love and care for him with all your heart and being, that you will melt his heart and you will have the rewarding result a wonderful, loving, and happy marriage. It is all worth it all.

The responsibilities of a married couple rest with both the husband and the wife. The Bible teaches the duties of each partner. With the Holy Ghost working in your life and God, you can have a Very Exciting and Happy Marriage the rest of your lives.

THREE

A Message to All Wives

DEAR WOMEN OF GOD, THE LORD MAY BE GROOMING YOU TO BE AN APOSTLE, PRESIDING BISHOP, BISHOP, PASTOR, ASSISTANT PASTOR, PROPHET, ELDER, EVANGELIST, MINISTER, OR DEACON WIFE.

PLEASE PONDER THESE NEXT INSTRUTIONS IN YOUR HEART.

Now we are going directly to the Bible to help you be the Holy Wife God wants you to be.

One of the things that is going to help your career and job as a wife of the Man of God ministry is a hand out of your job description. If you love God, your husband, and his ministry, this job description will not be hard to follow.

FOUR

A Bishop's Wife's Qualifications

Bishop's Wife: (**I Timothy 3:1-7, KJV**) You should have the same **Qualifications** as the **Bishop**; it will make your life easier. (**I will replace he or him and put you.**)

(I Timothy 3:2-5, KJV)

1. You should be **blameless. Blameless means** you should not be the cause of blame, discredit, or disgrace, that is not capable of sinning or liable to sin, free from fault and blame, a perfect reputation. You should not be causing trouble in the home, church, public, or anywhere.

2. You should be the wife of **one husband** and **faithful** to your husband.

3. You should be **Vigilant. Vigilant** means keeping careful watch for possible danger or difficulties. To carefully notice problems or signs of danger and to also be temperate, which means self-control. Moderation in action, thought, or feeling.

(1 Peter 5:8, KJV)

[8] Be sober, be vigilant; because your adversary the devil, as a roaring lion, walketh about, seeking whom he may devour:

You should be spiritually sober; not intoxicated or controlled by fleshly lust and carnal desires.

4. You should be **sober.** Sober means to be sound minded; that is, marked by temperance, moderation, or seriousness. You should show no excessive or extreme qualities of fancy, emotion, or prejudice but serious and possessing good judgment. To be sober means to have or show a very serious attitude or quality.

5.You should be **of good behavior.** Of good behavior means orderly in life, habits, and work. Good behavior at home, church, and in public.

6. You should be **given to hospitality. Given to hospitality means** given to generous and cordial reception of guests. To save in finances you may have to give dinner parties, and/or entertain other Clergy in your home during revivals. You have to make them feel at home.

7. You should be able to **teach the word**. Your husband may get sick, go out of town, or need to leave the church with someone he can trust. That might be you when no one else is available. Bishops and Pastors have left the wrong person in charge and when they came back the church was torn apart. So, study the word so you can teach a lesson and operate the ministry.

(2 Timothy 2:15, KJV): Study to shew thyself approved unto God, a workman that needeth not to be ashamed, **rightly dividing the word of truth**.

Every Christian must study the Bible. It is very important, but **(2 Timothy 2:15, KJV)** is **not** just a command to study the Bible. Being an approved workman involves much more! Timothy had to understand, study the word of God, and be diligent in his service to God. As a woman married to a **Man in ministry,** it is our duty to earnestly apply yourself in service to the Lord and your husband. Whatever he needs, you are his **HELP MEET**. When teaching from the Bible, you need the Holy Ghost to guide you in studying the word. Therefore, you will not be ashamed as you stand before God on the day of judgment.

(**1 Peter 3:15, KJV**) - But sanctify the Lord God in your hearts: and **[be] ready always** to **[give] an answer to every man that asketh you a reason of the hope that is in you** with meekness and fear.

(**Matthew 24:44, KJV**) - Therefore **be ye also ready**: for in such an hour as ye think not the Son of man cometh.

Also, you never know when your husband will ask you to teach Bible Class, he may have had a stressful day, his regular Bible Class Teacher may not show up or call in advance to tell him. You are always his backup system. Therefore, **be also ready to teach or preach.** If you are a preacher, never go to a Holy Convocation, Women Convention, or any Big Service without studying the word and have a message in your heart. Special Speaker's sometimes do not show up or the Bishop or whoever is in charge may be led by God to let you speak. **BE READY AT ALL TIMES.**

8. **Not given to wine**, you should not be addicted to alcohol. Do not drink any kind of alcoholic drink.

9. You should not be a **striker** or physically violent. Do not fight with your hands or tongue when you teach, preach, or at any time.

10. You should **not be greedy of filthy lucre**. **Greedy of filthy lucre** means love money so much you will not pay your tithes or give freely to the work of the Lord or needy people. Also, being greedy of filthy lucre means you love money so much until you will get it dishonestly.

11. You must be **patient**. **Patient means** to able to accept or tolerate delays, problems, or suffering without becoming annoyed or anxious, your time will come.

Synonyms of **patient**: (1) forbearing, uncomplaining, tolerant, long-suffering, resigned, calm composed, serene, even -tempered, tranquil, unexcitable, accommodating, understanding, kind, considerate, cool, persevering, persistent, diligent, determined, purposeful.

(2) The quality or being patient bearing of provocation, annoyance, misfortune, or pain without complaint, loss of temper, irritation, or the like an ability or willingness to suppress restlessness or annoyance when confronted with delay. Quiet, steady perseverance, and even-tempered care. In the former sense it is a quality of **self-restraint** or of **not giving way to anger**, even in the face of provocation. **Provocation** means action or speech that makes someone annoyed or angry, especially deliberately.

You should remain calm and not respond to provocation. Church people and church meetings can really get you so upset, but you must always remain calm and pray. You are going to have to endure a lot of heart ache and heart break because of the ministry and church people. God will not leave you or forsake you. Take your heart aches, heart breaks, and many tears to the Lord. Do your crying at home on your knees before God. Do not let the Church People see you cry; they will deliberately cause you to cry even more if they find out your soft spot. Therefore, keep your soft spot, crying, and anger between you and God.

(Psalm 39: 1 -7, KJV): I said, I will take heed to my ways, that I sin not with my tongue: I will keep my mouth with a bridle, while the wicked is before me. (2) I was dumb with silence, I held my peace, even from good; and my sorrow was stirred.

In the Church World people can really hurt the wife of a man in ministry if you let them. Remember everyone in the Church World is not sweetly saved or saved. Some of them will fight you because they don't normally fight the Great Men of God. Stay prayed and fasted up so you will not make God, your husband, or other church members ashamed if you lose your temper. Say what you mean without anger. Once you say something out your mouth, you can not take it back. You have to have self-restraint, forebear, and endure a lot of things for the sake of your position. It takes the Holy Ghost to help you. You have to make sure you do not sin with your tongue. You have to be silent and hold your peace even if you are right. You can be right and want to say something good but it may not be the right time.

Also, you must be **patient** with your husband's ministry. Every gifted, anointed, chosen Man of God is not going to have a **MEGA-CHURCH MINISTRY**. That was so hard for me. That is something that really bothered me. I just could not understand it. My husband has the characteristics of Jesus Christ. He has the pure Love of God for all people. He loves his enemies as well as his friends. He is blameless. I am his only wife, he treated me like a Queen, and my daughter like a Princess. He is vigilant, sober, of good behavior, given to hospitality, and apt to teach and highly anointed preacher. He has never been greedy over money. He is the most honest man I have ever met. The bank accidently gave him over $5,000.00 cash at the teller window, when we were in a financial hardship, yet he took the money back to the bank. He is not greedy of filthy lucre. He has gone out of town many times and preached to two people or a few people. He would preach like he was preaching to thousands. My husband has the patience of Job in the Bible. He is not a brawler and not covetous. He ruled his own house very well. He had his family in subjection with all gravity. I have been married to him for forty-seven years and I have found no fault in him.

My husband has all nine gifts from God, he had the pure love of God in his heart, he was highly anointed, and if possible, could preach the paint off the walls. I saw the greatness in my husband and he only had a small ministry. That was so hard for me. That is something that really bothered me. I just could not understand it. This really upset me. Every woman alive wants to see her husband be successful in his career. Only my husband career was in the ministry being a Pastor, a Bishop, and finally a Presiding Bishop. People would come to our church, get saved, get on their feet, and leave. I felt if my husband was the one that you got saved under, why can't you stay under him? Every time our church would get large, some would leave. One day a Bishop from another country called and said, "he wanted to fly over, come to my house, and talk to me." He told me, "I came all the way from another country to give you a **WORD FROM THE LORD**". The **WORD FROM THE LORD** was, "that my husband was already successful to God, because he was doing what God told him to do." The small number of people in your church, has nothing to do with being Successful with God.

Then another messenger from the Lord told me, "your Husband's Ministry is a **TRAINING STATION.** These people are not going to stay**, they get their training from your husband and leave to do great things for the Lord."** I was not really excited about that; however, I accepted the will of God. Most of the people that left our church they were well trained under our ministry and became great Apostles, Presiding Bishops, Bishops, Pastors, Elders, Evangelists, Ministers and/or wives of these great men. Also, some of the woman became Pastors of churches or married someone in ministry. You have to except what God allows and what He has ordained for your husband's ministry.

12. You can not be a **brawler. A brawler means** a person that loves to quarrel. You should be easy to overlook minor issues and problems. You can not be a person that must have it your way.

13. You can not be **covetous. Covetous means** desiring wealth or possessions that belong to another. **There will be many people or women that will come to your Husband's Church that will**

always have more money, clothes, bigger houses, and brand-new cars. Some members will get a new car every two years. You can not get angry and start desiring what they possess. You are an Apostle, Presiding Bishop, Bishop, Pastor, Prophet, Elder, Minister, Evangelist, or a Deacon's Wife; your husband will not normally make a lot of money in Full-Time Ministry unless he is over a Mega-Church. Your Husband will always give to the ministry more than anyone else. You must learn to be content with that fact and what you have.

(II Corinthians 9:7, KJV) Every man according as he purposeth in his heart, so let him give; not grudgingly, or of necessity: for God loveth a cheerful giver. **GRUDGINGLY MEANS IN A RELUCTANT OR RESENTFUL MANNER.**

God does not want our giving to be done **grudgingly**. You should not be reluctant, regretful, and complaining what you or your husband gave.

I was brought up poor, but blessed. I lived a Very Happy Life with my family. My mother and father were both filled with the Holy Ghost and made wonderful memories for me. We all ate together, went to church, prayed, played, and had fun family activities, and were happy together. My Mom, my Dad, and my First Pastor taught us to be happy for other people when they got blessed. This is the reason I am not jealous of anyone's blessings.

(Roman 12:15, KJV): Rejoice with them that do rejoice, and weep with them that weep.

Way back (in the 50's and 60's) most people in my church were poor. Even the Pastor lived in an apartment and had no car. When someone in the church got a car, after church, the congregation would go outside to see it; and rejoiced! My parents never bought a car or home. I was nineteen when I bought my first used mustang car. I loved it and everyone at the church was so proud of me buying a car. Most of the people that attended church in the (50's and 60's) lived in apartments. When someone was blessed with a house, the whole church would go over to their house give God the praise, and rejoice with them. So, most of my life my family and I would be excited and rejoicing over other people's blessings, houses, and cars. That same spirit is with me today. If you are happy with Jesus and your family there is no need to be covetous over anything anyone has. Jesus and a Happy Family Life is Priceless! As the years went by, God began to really bless the saints of God with prosperity. My family and I still rejoiced with them! You must learn as a wife of a man in ministry that Happiness does not come from having a lot of money or material things. First, it comes from having the Holy Ghost and being fervent in the Spirit. **(Fervent** means having a passionate intensity).

My first Pastor told me to always pray and tarry like you do not have the Holy Ghost. If you pray, tarry, and fast, you will be able to do His will and lead God's People.

(Acts 18:25, KJV)

> This man was instructed in the way of the Lord; and **being fervent in the spirit,** he spake and taught diligently the things of the Lord, knowing only the baptism of John.

(Romans 12:11, KJV) |

> Not slothful in business; **fervent in spirit**; serving the Lord;

(**Philippians 4:11-13, KJV**) - Not that I speak in respect of want: for I have learned, in whatsoever state I am, [therewith] **to be content**.

(**Hebrews 13:5, KJV**) - [Let your] conversation [be] **without covetousness**; [and be] **content with such things as ye have**: for he hath said, I will never leave thee, nor forsake thee.

(**1 Timothy 6:6-8, KJV**) - But **godliness with** contentment is **great gain**.

Content means a state of **PEACEFUL HAPPINESS**. To be satisfied, and free from care because of satisfaction. *A Permanent state of mind of Peace and Happiness.*

Content also means to be free from care because of satisfaction with what is already one's own.

You do not have to have anything to happen to cause you to be Happy because you already have JESUS. He gives you joy that the world does not have. Look at the movie stars, celebrities, millionaires, and billionaires that kill themselves. They have everything that this world can give them but are not happy! Contentment comes from God and is Priceless!

If you do not learn to have joy with small things, you will never be happy with a lot. God wants us to give *happily* because that is how God Himself gives. True giving *comes* from a cheerful heart and it also *gives* us a happy heart.

Now, I love to give to the Work of the Lord also. Yet, I have not reached the limit of my husband's giving. That may never happen; however, I do not speak about how he gives or help people. I still believe he goes beyond the call of duty. He is a Great Man of God and obeys God no matter what.

The most important thing Our Savior is looking at in your giving is the attitude in which you are giving rather than with the amount that you give. The Lord wants a willing attitude from givers.

(II Corinthians 9:6, KJV)

But this I say, He which soweth sparingly shall reap also sparingly; and he which soweth bountifully shall reap also bountifully.

Therefore, I am giving you scriptures in the word of God to back up how **Men of God** give, how we must condition ourselves, and bow to the will of God. No matter what The **Man of God** gives, say Amen. When we get this attitude God will reap blessings that are both natural and spiritual. God will provide for the cheerful giver.

(Philippians 4:19, KJV)

But my God shall supply all your need according to his riches in glory by Christ Jesus.

(Matthew 19:29, KJV): [29] And every one that hath forsaken houses, or brethren, or sisters, or father, or mother, or wife, or children, or lands, for my name's sake, shall receive a hundredfold, and shall inherit everlasting life.

I've experienced forty-seven years of transition of being a Minister's, Elder's, Pastor's, Bishop's, and currently a Presiding Bishop's wife, I can promise you that you will make billions of sacrifices for the ministry! However, I also will confirm that God will supply your every need. He will reward you in ways that you will not expect! That would be another Book. He will reward you now and in eternity! You cannot out give our Lord and Savior!

14. You must **rule your own house well**.

A. Rule your own house well means being a woman whose main occupation is caring for her family which makes her a housewife/ Domestic Engineer. A Housewife is a woman who has chosen to not work outside the home for money, but rather devotes all time, energy and love into creating a safe, warm, clean home for her family to grow and thrive. She cooks, cleans, does dishes, laundry, childcare, shopping, countless errands, and carefully manages money all while supporting her family. Commonly referred to as a <u>stay at home mom</u> or <u>homemaker</u>. A Domestic Engineer stay at home-mom stays at her home during the day (unemployed), usually with her husband supporting the family financially. However, times have changed so that most women have to do what a house wife does and also hold down a full-time job. I take my hat off to these women; they are WONDER WOMEN!

B. Having your children in subjection with **<u>all gravity</u>**.

<u>Gravity</u> means:

1: the quality or state of being dignified and proper

2: The quality or state of being important or serious.

<u>(Ephesians 6:1, KJV)</u>

Children, obey your parents in the Lord, for this is right.

<u>(Ephesians 6:1-4, KJV)</u>

Children, obey your parents in the Lord, for this is right. "Honor your father and mother" (this is the first commandment with a promise), "that it may go well with you and that you may live long in the land." Fathers, do not provoke your children to anger, but bring them up in the discipline and instruction of the Lord.

You are the mother, not the children. You must train your children to obey you. That is your job not leaving it to teachers to raise your children. You are the first authority figure in your child's life. It takes a lot of time to train a child, but it is our responsibility. I know you love your child. Train your child to respect authority so they can live a long life. You have to discipline and instruct your child.

Start with them when they are young to respect and obey you. Teach them to sit quiet at home. Have a quiet time every day. You are training them to sit for church and school. When they are small you dress them to look dignified and proper. This is a GREAT GIFT I am going to give you; another mother of three girls helped me out with this. Pre-adolescence, also known as pre-teen or tween, is a stage of human development following early childhood and preceding adolescence. It commonly ends with the beginning of puberty but may also be defined as ending with the start of the teenage years. For example, the age range is commonly designated as 10–13 years. When you daughter or son become 10- 13 they are becoming into pre-adolescence and they will change. They will not like any of the clothes you pick out. To be in control, take them to the store and let them pick out their own clothes. Tell them your requirements such as the length and size, to refrain from clothes that are too tight, or sexy. With your supervision, they can still look dignified and still be in style with the time. We as mothers must understand that when they become pre-teens, our styles are old fashioned. They are growing up! Let them respect and obey you but let them mature. You do not want them to stay on pampers and drink out of a milk bottle the rest of their lives.

Also, you can not out talk or yell at a pre-teen. Their little brains are faster than yours. You re-establish your rules of respect when they become a pre-teen. Tell them you still can not yell or raise your voice at MOTHER. Write me a letter how you feel explaining that I am unfair. Ninety-nine % (99%) of the time as they write the letter, they will see they are unreasonable and you the mother is right. My children became great writers in school because of this. Also, if you have a high-spirited female for a daughter you must learn the "HAND TRICK". When they refuse to shut up, lift your "HAND" in their face and say "THIS CONVERSATION IS OVER GO TO YOUR ROOM "and write!

During this time, we "THE MOTHER" are the enemy. Dad is not home; he is at work or doing ministry. So, we are the "VILLIAINS "that say no to this and that. Do not worry, it will pass, it's hormones. A lot of children during pre-teen will try to bring confusion between mother and father. Do not let them do it. All the husband has to say to your children is "YOU HAVE TO OBEY YOUR MOM AND HER RULES BECAUSE I AM AT WORK MOST OF THE TIME. DO NOT COME TO ME FOR A DIFFERENT ANSWER, JUST DO WHAT YOUR MOTHER SAYS." Again, this time of your child life will pass and things will get better.

Also, you must let your children know you love them until they never have doubt about it. Hug them and kiss them always. Teenagers need hugs and kisses even more. They really go through a lot at school! You go check on them at school frequently, have daily talks with your children to see how they feel, always tell you children that they can tell you anything even if they have done wrong. Have a confession time with your children throughout their lives. Confession time is when they tell things they done wrong and you promise them you will not punish them for it. You tell momma, momma is your friend and if you are in trouble, momma is going try to help you. Nurture them to let them know you are their best friend. It is our responsibility to care for and encourage the growth and development of our children. It is our assignment to examine them to see if they are head-strong, stubborn, selfish, or any other characteristics that will hinder them in life. It is our job to heal, cure, and destroy these characteristics when they are very young. You can not bend a full-grown tree.

15. For if a woman knows not how to rule her own house, how shall she help take care of the church of God? If a Bishop's or Pastor's wife does not know how to rule her own house, (**not rule your husband**, but rule your children and have your house in order) how can she help her husband to take care of the church of God?

16. Not a novice: **Novice** means you are not a beginner in the service of the Lord or she may be lifted up with pride and she will fall.

17. She must have a **good report of people that are poor** or **misfortunate**. Your husband will assist people that you think are not worthy to be helped. However, never tell your husband not to give or help someone. He is a **Man of God** and it will take a lot of prayer and fasting to try to understand a **Man of God's** giving. You may never understand it. You will feel people are taking advantage of your husband and that is not the case. He may be on a higher and different level than you, when it comes to helping the poor and misfortunate. Be quiet and pray, but if God reveals something to you that isn't right about a situation, come to your husband in a sweet humble spirit.

When I was only nineteen, my husband called a Preacher from another state to come and preach at our church. He brought his whole family; we gave them our bedrooms and we slept on the floor. After, he ran a revival for our church his car broke down and he did not have enough money to fix his car to go home. My husband gave him our mortgage payment to fix his car and the preacher was able to fix his car and go home with his family. My husband did not know how he was going to replace the money for our house mortgage. He just prayed and believed God will provide and make a way. The mortgage company sent us a letter that we had paid too much in our mortgage escrow account and we did not have to pay mortgage that month! Also, they reduced the remaining payments for our mortgage. A **Man of God** like my husband has AWESOME TREMENDOUS FAITH. LOOK AT GOD! I could tell you many examples when my husband stepped out on faith and God came to his rescue each time! Sometimes I had to just hold my breath and pray as he helped the poor, the misfortunate, and the unbelievable things he did to maintain our first real church building.

18. She must be a **cheerful giver** and **support the poor; so, <u>he will not fall into reproach and a snare of the devil</u>**. You have to be happy to give to the work of the Lord. You have to become a cheerful giver and support the church and the poor.

My husband was a cheerful giver and he would do anything to enhance or promote the Work of the Lord. I was nineteen when my husband started his own church from scratch. Therefore, my husband had to pay the Church rent, vepco, water, and everything from his pocket for years. My mother told me do not come between my husband and God. Therefore, I did a lot of praying, fasting, and had a quiet spirit to endure how my husband gave money to the Work of the Lord.

To buy his first church he borrowed thirty-three thousand from the bank and got three personal loans in our name to purchase the church. We paid all of the loans off way before time. Look at God! The city of Norfolk told us that they had to tear our church down, and we had to move. My husband used our house, everything in our house, and our two cars as collateral to get loans to buy our second church. The bank's Finance Officer asked me did I understand that if my husband did not make the

payments, the bank will come and take my house, all the items in my house, and both of our cars. The bank finance officer asked me was I alright? I was not alright! I was scared to death that we would lose everything we owned. However, I would not say anything negative to my husband or to the bank officer. I just nodded my head and continued to look out the window until all the signing of the papers were over.

B. **Reproach** means to address (someone) in such a way as to express disapproval or disappointment.

(1 Timothy 3:7, KJV)

7 And he must have a good reputation with those outside the church, that are non-believers, so that he will not fall into reproach or disgrace and be caught by the devil's trap.

What is the meaning of "reproach and snare of the Devil"?

We as Christians are always inviting unbelievers to attend our congregation's meetings.

Just imagine the reaction of a Non-Christian walking into the congregation and noticing an Apostle, Presiding Bishop, Bishop, Pastor, Prophet, Elder, Minister, Evangelist, or Deacon that own's a business and was cheating him at his work with his wages. Having a fine reputation with Non-Christians would prevent a Pastor or his wife from being exposed to a scandal or get caught in the devil's snare.

EXAMPLE: You are in the ministry; you may be a supervisor or owner of a business. You do not pay your employees on time, under minimum wages, do not let them have breaks and just give them a short time to eat lunch, work them in unsafe environments, make them work overtime and do not pay them for overtime, do not give your employees vacation time, employees get sick and you will not let them go home, being unusual cruel to your employees.

Then some one on the job call the government and fill out a report on the unlawful deeds you are doing. Then there is a government investigation and you have a scandal on TV. When you do wrong as a Christian or Church leader the devil will make sure it will come advertised so he can catch you in a snare as a hunter catches an animal in a trap.

A man in the ministry have a scandal about something he did unlawful, it gives him a bad reputation in the community, the local church, and such a scandal damages the faith they represent as well.

FIVE

A DEACON'S WIVES QUALIFICATIONS

DEACON WIVES: (I Timothy 3:8,11,12, KJV) **If you are a Deacon Wife. (I will replace he or him and put you.)** You should have the same qualification as the deacon, it will make your life easier.

1. You must be **grave**. **Grave means:** 1: Deserving serious consideration. 2: Dignified in appearance or manner, serious, solemn. Deacon wives must be grave.

2. You must **not be double-tongued**. Double-tongued is defined as being deceitful and hypocritical. Being double-tongued means to say one thing at one time to someone and another thing another time to someone else. To have a double tongue can also mean hypocritically saying one thing and doing another. The double-tongued will say what's expected in the moment, but speak differently when the person is not around. A double-tongued person is untrustworthy and lacks integrity. Double-tongue people want to please people by saying what they want them to hear, not intending to do it like Ananias and Sapphira in the bible **(Acts 5:1–11, KJV).** They told the disciples that they would sell their land and donate all the money to the church. They lied and they died because of being double-tongued.

As a deacon's wife you must always say what you mean and do what you say always. Do not seek to please people. As humans we can not please people. Just work on pleasing your husband and the Lord.

3. **Not given to wine**, you should not be addicted to alcohol. Do not drink any kind of alcoholic drink.

4. You should **not be greedy of filthy lucre**. **Greedy of filthy lucre** means love money so much you will not pay your tithes or give freely to the work of the Lord or those in need. Also, being greedy of filthy lucre means you love money so much until you will get it dishonestly. As a deacon's wife, your husband will handle most of the Church's money. Sometimes he has to take the money home to deposit money for the Pastor into the Church Account. You have to resist the devil at all times about Church Money. Never borrow God's money because the devil will make sure you can not pay it back. If the Church People hear this, it is over for your husband and you being a Deacon's wife. Do not let the love of money cause you to steal church money, it is not borrowing, it is stealing God's money. Do not ever do this. I can tell some stories about church financial meetings when the deacon, deacon's wife, treasure, or secretary borrowed Church Money and the Pastor called a Financial meeting and they can not come up with the money because they borrowed, (really stole God's money). They will be standing in front of the Church Meeting trying to tell the Church I was going to pay it back. When they are exposed in front of church in the meeting, their position was taken from them. That is embarrassing, the money is not the Deacon or the Pastor's money; it is God's Money to build the Kingdom.

5. You must **not be a slanderer**. **Slander means:** A false or untruthful report or charge; also, a **truth circulated with a hostile purpose**. The Bible contains **numerous warnings against tale-bearing**, **gossip**, and other forms of **evil-speaking**. Paul especially condemns slander, perhaps as a result of his experience with those who slandered him and his work.

(Leviticus 19:16, KJV)

Thou shalt not go up and down as a **talebearer among** thy people: neither shalt thou stand against the blood of thy neighbour: I am the LORD.

TALEBEARER is a person who **maliciously gossips** or **reveals secrets**.

As a deacon's wife you can not be a talebearer among your husband's church or any church, your job, or in your neighborhood. As a deacon's wife, the Pastor will send you and your husband to many people's homes to do the work of the Lord. You will find out a lot of private things about people such as where they live, their status financially, separations, divorces, fights, loss of jobs, sex offenders, them or their family members that have been convicted of Rape, Rape of a Child, Child Molestation, Sexual Misconduct with a Minor, Sexual Violation of Human Remains, Incest, and many other secrets. All these things you have to only report back to the Pastor and the Pastor will determine if police need to investigate. It is the Pastor's job to report new violations of the law to the police. You can not be a talebearer, even if it is true. A deacon is a helper and assistant to the Pastor. It is a very high position in the church because the Pastor has confidence in him to take care of church business. He is the Pastor's right-hand man. Something like the Vice-President of the USA. Being married to a deacon is a high position as a Deacon's Wife. Don't make God, your Pastor, your husband, and church members lose confidence in you. You will find out things about members of your church that will **shock** you, but you have to carry it to your Pastor and take that secret to the grave.

(Proverbs 11:13, KJV) |

A talebearer **revealeth secrets**: but he that is of a **faithful spirit concealeth the matter**.

(Proverbs 18:8, KJV) |

The words of a **talebearer** are as **wounds** and they go down into the **innermost parts of the belly.**

(I Peter 3:10-11, KJV)

[10] For he that will love life, and see good days, let him **refrain his tongue from evil**, and **his lips that they speak no guile:**

[11] Let him **eschew evil**, and do good; let him seek peace, and ensue it.

You can not be a **GOSSIPER**. You can not go around your husband's church, other churches, your job, or in your neighborhood spreading details true or not. If you cannot spread details that you know are true, certainly the Lord does not want you to spread details that are not confirmed as being true. It is hard for a woman to keep silent on juicy gossip, but you must because of the word of God and your high position in the church. Yes, you are very important in the church because you reflect the Godliness of your husband with your actions. Many deacons have been fired because of the behavior of their wives. You do not want to disgrace God, your Pastor, and certainly not your husband. Fast and pray for a meek and quiet spirit. In the sight of God, it is a **GREAT PRICE**.

(I Peter 3:4, KJV)

But let it be the hidden man of the heart, in that which is not corruptible, even the ornament of **a meek and quiet spirit**, which **is in the sight of God of great price**.

(Ephesians 4:29, KJV)

Let no corrupt communication proceed out of your mouth, but that which is good to the use of edifying, that it may minister grace unto the hearers.

Slanderers, talebearers, gossipers, and women that engage in all forms of evil speaking do not edify the church or anyone. People that are trying to keep family secrets have committed suicide or killed people for revealing their family secrets. Many people have left the church over slanderers, talebearers, gossipers, and evil speaking of them. They believe all Christians are alike and never step in a church again! That is very dangerous, causing a soul to be lost because you could not keep confidential secrets. We've all heard the saying **Sticks** and **Stones** may break my bones but **WORDS** will never hurt me. This is not true. Words, true or false have hurt many people and scarred them for the rest of their lives. Look at some of those talk shows on TV. Things people or children said to them when they were young has still affected their whole life and them.

6. You must be **Sober: Sober means** Habitual temperance (self-control), Sobriety has reference to temperance of thought and action, calmness, seriousness, gravity, etc.

7. You must be **Faithful in all things;** Faithful in attending church, choir, usher, auxiliaries, paying tithes, offerings, raising your children, and being a good wife. Always be **Faithful in keeping church rules.**

8. You must have one husband. Let the deacons be the husbands of one wife, ruling their children, and their own homes well.

9. For if a woman knows not how to rule her own house, how shall she help take care of the church of God? If a Deacon's wife does not know how to rule her own house, (**not rule your husband**, but rule your children and have your house in order) how can she help her husband to take care of the church of God?

You must **rule your own house well**. It means being a woman whose main occupation is caring for her family which makes her a housewife. A Housewife or Domestic Engineer is a woman who has chosen to not work outside the home for money, but rather devotes all time, energy, and love into the home. She creates a safe, warm, clean home for her family to grow and thrive. The woman cooks, cleans, does dishes, laundry, childcare, shopping, countless errands. She also helps with money management while supporting her family. Commonly referred to as a stay at home mom or homemaker. A Domestic Engineer stays at her home during the day (unemployed), usually with her husband supporting the family financially. However, times have changed so that most woman have to do what a house wife does and also hold down a full-time job. I take my hat off to these women; they are **WONDER WOMAN**!

SIX

An Elders's Wife and All Other Clergy Wives

(Titus 2:3-5, KJV) Aged women teach good things to the young women.

1. **Behavior as becometh Holiness**
2. **Not false accusers (not slanderers)**
3. **Not given to Wine: Do not drink alcohol**
4. **Teachers of Good things**
5. **Sober:** Make a habit of controlling yourself at home, in public, and especially at church. Not addicted to drinking alcohol, smoking, or drugs. Be calm, temperance, use moderation, or seriousness, showing no excess or extreme qualities.
6. **Love your husbands. Love your husband until he never doubts your love.**
7. **Love your children. Love your children until they never doubt your love.**
8. **To be discreet:** having or showing good judgment especially in conduct or speech. Capable of preserving silence and being able to avoid causing offense or to gain an advantage.
9. **Chaste:** pure in thought and act: modest, spotless, simple, or plain in design. We cannot wear every new style that comes out. Dress like you are going to church not a night club.
10. **Keepers at home:** You, your home, your children, and your husband should always be clean and neat. You should not preach or teach unless your home is clean and everything

is happy at home. Charity begins at home. **(Proverbs 31: 10-31, KJV)**

11. **Good**: of a favorable character or tendency, agreeable, pleasant, virtuous, just, loyal, and reliable. God, the pastor, your husband, your children, and your church should be able to rely on you. Keep your word. Example: When you are scheduled to work a job in the church. Show up faithfully. If an emergency arrives, call the church ahead of time and explain the problem.

12. **Obedient to their own husbands**: Obey your own husbands. It looks so ugly to pay attention to everyone else's husband and ignore your own.

13. **Obedient to their own husbands, that the word of God be not blasphemed. Blasphemed** means to disrespect or dishonor God. Obeying your own husband and how you act at home is very important to God. Home life must be right or you'll be disrespecting and dishonoring God.

SEVEN

Virtous Women

All Wives should be (Virtuous Women).

VIRTURE: A POSITIVE TRAIT OR QUALITY DEEMED TO BE MORALLY GOOD AND CONFORMITY TO A STANDARD OF RIGHT. CONFORMITY OF ONE'S LIFE AND CONDUCT TO MORAL AND ETHICAL PRINCIPLES. THE QUALITY OR PRACTICE OF MORAL EXCELLENCE OR RIGHTEOUSNESS, GOODNESS, UPRIGHTNESS, ANY ADMIRABLE QUALITY, FEATURE OR TRAIT, COURAGE; A CAPACITY TO ACT. CHASTITY ESP. IN WOMEN.

MAKE VIRTURE A NECESSITY AS A WIFE OF MEN OF GOD: TO ACCEPT, SUBMIT, COMPLY SILENTLY OR WITHOUT A PROTEST, AND AGREE IN DOING SOMETHING UNPLEASANT WITH A SHOW OF GRACE BECAUSE ONE MUST DO IT IN ANY CASE.

(PROVERBS 31:10-31, KJV) A VIRTUOUS WOMAN, HER PRICE IS FAR ABOVE RUBIES.

1. HER HUSBAND SAFELY TRUST IN HER
2. SHE WILL DO HIM GOOD ALL THE DAYS OF HIS LIFE (NOT EVIL)
3. WORKETH WILLINGLY WITH HER HANDS WITH HOUSEWORK
4. SHE BRINGETH FOOD FROM AFAR (NO FAST FOOD). BUY YOUR MEATS IN BIG QUANTITY, YOU WILL GET MORE FOR LESS.

5. SHE RISETH EARLY-DO NOT STAY IN BED ALL DAY.
6. SHE FEEDS HER HOUSEHOLD (BREAKFAST, LUNCH, AND DINNER)
7. CANDLE GOETH NOT OUT BY NIGHT, (NOT LAZY) BUSY
8. IN THE 21ST CENTURY, SHE SEWS AND GOES TO (YARD SALES, THRIFT STORES) TO KEEP COST DOWN.
9. SHE HELPS THE POOR AND NEEDY.
10. SHE IS NOT AFRAID OF WINTER FOR HER HOUSEHOLD. SHE IS PREPARED YEAR ROUND. SHE WILL WORK HARD FOR HER FAMILY NO MATTER WHAT THE WEATHER.
11. HER HOUSEHOLD IS CLOTHED WITH SCARLET. HER CHILDREN & HUSBAND DRESS WELL.
12. SHE MAKES HERSELF COVERINGS OF TAPESTRY (TASPESTRY WAS SOLD TO DECORATE PALACES, CASTLES, AND MOST VALUABLE MATERIAL WOVEN WITH GOLD). HER CLOTHING IS FINE SILK, AND PURPLE. SHE DRESSES WELL.
13. HER HUSBAND IS KNOWN IN THE GATES WHEN HE SITTETH AMONG THE ELDERS OF THE LAND. SHE WILL MAKE SURE HE IS WELL GROOMED AT ALL TIMES, ESPECIALLY WHEN HE GOES TO CHURCH. HE LOOKS AND SMELL GOOD AT CHURCH OR IN PUBLIC
14. SHE MAKES FINE LINEN AND GIRDLES TO SELL.
15. STRENGTH AND HONOR ARE HER CLOTHING AND SHE REJOICE IN TIME TO COME.
16. SHE OPENS HER MOUTH WITH WISDOM AND SHE IS KIND.
17. SHE TAKES GOOD CARE OF HER HOUSEHOLD AND IS NOT IDLE.

18. HER CHILDREN RISE UP AND CALL HER BLESSED AND HER HUSBAND WILL PRAISE HER.
19. SHE FEARETH THE LORD AND SHE IS PRAISED.
20. HER OWN WORKS PRAISE HER IN THE GATES (HEAVEN'S GATES).

EIGHT

THE THINGS MY FIRST PASTOR TAUGHT ME, (HOW TO BE A GOOD SAVED WIFE).

1. BE FAITHFUL TO GOD
2. ALWAYS GO TO CHURCH NO MATTER WHAT HAPPENS IN YOUR LIFE
3. DO NOT JUMP FROM CHURCH TO CHURCH, STAY WHERE GOD PLANTED YOU SO YOU CAN GROW
4. FAST, PRAY, AND TARRY TO BE FERVENT IN THE SPIRIT.
5. NEVER FIGHT OR FUSS OVER THE GOSPEL OR TRY TO DEFEND THAT GOD SENT YOU TO PREACH AS A WOMAN
6. ALWAYS KEEP A CLEAN HOUSE AND COOK HOME COOKED MEALS FOOD FOR YOUR HUSBAND AND FAMILY; NO FAST FOOD.
7. RESPECT YOUR HUSBAND AND BE KIND TO HIM EVERY DAY. DON'T RAISE YOUR VOICE AT HIM, ALWAYS SMILE AND SAY GOOD MORNING HONEY!
8. IF YOU ARE HAVING TROUBLE WITH YOUR CHILDREN, LAY ACROSS THEIR BEDS, FAST, PRAY, AND TELL JESUS ABOUT IT. A CHANGE WILL COME.
9. DRESS AS BECOMING HOLINESS AND GODLINESS

On our 47th Anniversary, Sunday, January 3, 2021, my husband introduced me to the church before I preached. The wonderful things he said about me were AWESOME. All because of my first Pastor's teaching. She is still a GREAT WOMAN OF GOD. She taught me so many things such as no matter what, stand still, go to church, and it will work out! I have a wonderful life because she taught me these things listed above. Because of her, I am happily married to the (GREATEST HUSBAND IN THE WORLD).

I have not ever forgotten how much she poured into me. I am so thankful for her being a Special Pastor, Mother, and (WOMAN OF GOD). She taught me how to follow her example.

NINE

AGED WOMEN TEACH ALL WOMEN ESPECIALLY THE YOUNG WOMEN

(TITUS 2:1-15, KJV)

(Titus 2:1, KJV)

But speak thou the things which become sound doctrine:

SOUND: FREE FROM FLAW, DEFECT, DECAY, OR ERROR; LOGICALLY VALID AND HAVING TRUE PREMISES, SOLID AND FIRM.

SOUND DOCTRINE: LITTERALLY, THAT WHICH IS TAUGHT. THE TERM MAY REFER TO ANY SPECIAL CODE OR SYSTEM OF RELIGION, MORALS, ETHICS OR PRINCIPLES TAUGHT OR DELIVERED; SUCH AS CATHOLIC DOCTRINE, PRESBYTERIAN DOCTRINE, BAPTIST DOCTRINE, AND APOSTOLIC DOCTRINE. THE CHRISTIAN DOCTRINE IS BASED ON THE PREACHING AND WRITING OF JESUS AND HIS APOSTOLES. THE NEW TESTAMENT CONTAINS NUMEROUS WARNINGS AGAINST FALSE DOCTRINES.

(ACTS 2:42, KJV) AND THEY CONTINUED STEDFASTLY IN THE APOSTOLES' DOCTRINE AND FELLOWSHIP, AND IN BREAKING OF BREAD, AND IN PRAYERS.

(TITUS 2:3-15, KJV)

3 The aged <u>women</u> <u>likewise,</u> that they be <u>in</u> <u>behaviour</u> as becometh <u>holiness,</u> <u>not</u> false <u>accusers,</u> <u>not</u> <u>given</u> to <u>much</u> <u>wine,</u> teachers of good <u>things;</u>

I am an aged woman. I am a Sixty-six-year-old woman that's been filled up with the Holy Ghost since I was twelve years old. My behavior exemplifies holiness, not a false accuser. I do not drink any kind of wine or alcoholic drink. I am teaching <u>Good Things</u> in this Chapter to all women, especially to the young, saved women. I have been teaching for over thirty years.

I often tell people that I am a Proverbs 31 and Titus Chapter 2 Woman. I can teach because I live what I teach. God chose me to teach all women.

<u>(II PETER 1:12 & 13, KJV):</u>

[12] Wherefore I will not be negligent to put you always in remembrance of these things, though ye know them, and be established in the present truth.

[13] Yea, I think it meet, as long as I am in this tabernacle, to stir you up by putting you in remembrance;

Peter told the church he would not be negligent (failing to take proper care in doing something), he would not fail to take proper care to continue to tell the church the truth. We had an elderly Church mother in our ministry that only taught on women until she died. She said, **<u>"ALWAYS KEEP THE TEACHING IN THE CHURCH".</u>** I have taken up this cross not to neglect teaching the women of God how to conduct themselves as Becometh Holiness. Peter told the people of God that you know what is right but I must always put you in remembrance of these things. Peter warns the Church that there are false teachers who are spreading wrong, and damaging doctrine. He warns them to keep a close watch on what you do in your personal life if you are saved.

(TITUS 2:4-15, KJV)

4 That they may teach the young women to be sober, to love their husbands, to love their children,

5 To be discreet, chaste, keepers at home, good, obedient to their own husbands, that the word of God be not blasphemed.

6 Young men likewise exhort to be sober minded.

7 In all things shewing thyself a pattern of good works: in doctrine shewing uncorruptness, gravity, sincerity,

8 Sound speech, that cannot be condemned; that he that is of the contrary part may be ashamed, having no evil thing to say of you.

10 Not purloining, but shewing all good fidelity; that they may adorn the doctrine of God our Saviour in all things.

11 For the grace of God that bringeth salvation hath appeared to all men,

12 Teaching us that, denying ungodliness and worldly lusts, we should live soberly, righteously, and godly, in this present world;

13 Looking for that blessed hope, and the glorious appearing of the great God and our Saviour Jesus Christ;

14 Who gave himself for us, that he might redeem us from all iniquity, and purify unto himself a peculiar people, zealous of good works.

15 These <u>things</u> <u>speak</u>, <u>and</u> <u>exhort</u>, <u>and</u> <u>rebuke</u> <u>with</u> <u>all</u> <u>authority</u>. <u>Let</u> no <u>man</u> <u>despise</u> <u>thee</u>.

(TITUS 2:4-10, KJV)

    1.   TEACH YOUNGER WOMEN TO BE SOBER

(I TIMOTHY 5:13, KJV) AND WITHAL THEY LEARN TO BE IDLE, WANDERING ABOUT FROM HOUSE TO HOUSE; AND NOT ONLY IDLE, BUT TATTLERS ALSO AND BUSYBODIES, SPEAKING THINGS WHICH THEY OUGHT NOT.

(I TIMOTHY 5:14, KJV) I WILL THEREFORE THAT THE YOUNGER WOMEN MARRY, BEAR CHILDREN, GUIDE THE HOUSE, GIVE NONE OCCASION TO THE ADVERSARY TO SPEAK REPROACHFULLY (express criticism, disgraceful, shameful).

    2. **SOBER**: NOT ADDICTED TO DRINK, SMOKING, OR DRUGS. CALM, TEMPERANCE, MODERATION OR SERIOUSNESS, SHOWING NO EXCESS OR EXTREME QUALITIES.
    3. LOVE THEIR HUSBANDS AND CHILDREN
    4. **TO BE DISCREET**: HAVING OR SHOWING DISCERNMENT OR GOOD JUDGMENT IN CONDUCT AND ESP. SPEECH. CAPABLE OF PRESERVING SILENCE, careful and circumspect in one's speech or actions, especially in order to avoid causing offense or to gain an advantage
    5. **CHASTE**: INNOCENT OF UNLAWFUL SEXUAL INTERCOURSE, CELIBATE, PURE IN THOUGHT AND ACT, MODEST, SEVERELY SIMPLE IN

DESIGN. WE CAN NOT WEAR EVERY STYLE THAT COMES OUT.

6. **KEEPERS AT HOME**: YOUNG WOMEN LIVING A GODLY LIFE MUST FIRST HAVE SELF-CONTROL, BE SENSIBLE, AND BE PURE. BUSY AT HOME BEING A HOMEMAKERS. THIS SCRIPTURE DOES NOT PROHIBIT WOMEN WORKING ANOTHER JOB OUTSIDE THE HOME. RATHER, PAUL IS TELLING WOMEN HOW IMPORTANT IT IS FOR CARING FOR THE HOME. GODLY WOMEN DO NOT STAY HOME ALL DAY LOOKING AT TV, TALKING ON THE PHONE, AND KEEPING A FILTHY HOME.

7. **GOOD**:

8. **OBEDIENT TO THEIR OWN HUSBANDS**:

(TITUS 2: 7-13, KJV)

(7). In all things **shewing thyself a pattern of good works**; in doctrine shewing incorruptness, **gravity, sincerity**.

(8). **Sound speech**, that cannot be condemned; that he that is of the contrary part may be ashamed, having no evil thing to say of you.

(10). **Not purloining, Purloining means** (stealing) Example: selling church candy, working in church kitchen, bake sales, collecting money for patrons list and spending the money for yourself, and never turning in the money to the church).

Fidelity :(the quality or state of being faithful, exactness in details) but **shewing all good fidelity**; that they may adorn the doctrine of God our Savior in all things. We must be faithful to God, our husbands, and our church.

(12). **Teaching us that, denying ungodliness and worldly lusts, we should live soberly, righteously, and godly, in this present world;**

(13) Looking for that blessed hope, and the glorious appearing of the great God and our Savior Jesus Christ;

(14) WHO GAVE HIMSELF FOR US, THAT HE MIGHT **REDEEM US FROM ALL INIQUITY**, AND **PURIFY UNTO HIMSELF** **A PECULIAR PEOPLE**, **ZEALOUS OF GOOD WORKS**.

(15) These things speak, and exhort, and rebuke with all authority. Let no man despise thee.

I must continue to teach women of God how to be Holy starting at home. We are living in a world that people feel it is right to do anything that feels good. However, if you want to see Jesus, and hear him say, "WELL DONE," you must deny ungodliness and worldly lust. Women must still do what the Bible expects of us. We must live soberly, righteously, and godly, in this present world.

TEN

How Thou Ought to Behave Thyself in the House of God.

(I Timothy 3:15, KJV) But if I tarry long, that **thou mayest know how thou oughtest to behave thyself in the house of God,** which is the church of the living God, the pillar and ground of the truth.

KNOW HOW THOU OUGHTEST TO BEHAVE THYSELF IN THE HOUSE OF GOD:

1. Rebuke not an elder, but intreat him as a father; and the younger men as brethren **(I Tim 5:1, KJV).** Let the elders that rule well be counted worthy of double honour, especially they who labour in the word and doctrine **(I Tim 5:17, KJV). REBUKE: TO CRITICIZE SHARPLY, AN EXPRESSION OF STRONG DISAPPROVAL.** It looks really ugly to stand up in God's house and criticize and express your strong disapproval of something or someone. Never to try to force your pastor, elder, deacon, anyone with authority, and especially your husband to accept your view. You express your opinion softly in a respectful way at home or in the Pastor's office. **If you love your husband and believe in his ministry, lift him up, give, and show honor to him. Sometimes you are your husband's only friend in the church. In the Church World people will always talk about the pastor. If anything goes wrong, it's the pastor's fault.**

- Do not yell, scream, fuss, or point your finger in your husband face, (immature)
- Do not yell at your children in public train them at home, (Have a quiet time at home and let them sit down so they will learn to sit at church or anywhere).
- Do not boss or order your husband like he is a little boy; you are not his mother, but his wife. He is God's man.
- Do not belittle your husband at home, and especially not in public.
- Do not go around looking like a bag lady after having children, keep yourself up.
- Do not talk about private things about your husband in public.
- Do not chew gum in church. It seems to be an epidemic with preachers, their wives, and especially members of the Music department. Honor God's house. Mints or hard candy is fine.
- Do not put female items all around bathroom, your bedroom, or other areas of the house. Keep your whole house clean, especially the living room, dining room, and kitchen. These are rooms that visitors see when they first come to your house. Always keep your bathroom clean. Friends, visitors, repair men, or anyone may need to go to the bathroom at any time.
- Ask your husband about how much he wants you to clean his study, man cave, or any room that he stays in a lot. These rooms are his domain. Do not get upset if he does not want you to clean it at all. Just be happy you have at least one room or area you do not have to clean. Just act as if it is not part of the house. Do not have any discussion, arguments, or fuss how he keeps it. It is his room, his domain, his private place to relax from the whole world. Most men are not open about things that trouble them. When he goes to his study,

man cave, or any room that he stays in a lot, "leave him alone". LEAVE HIM ALONE!!! He does not want anything to eat or drink. Just leave him alone. When he is relaxed, he will come out. A wise woman will learn this wonderful skill. He is trying to settle his nerves and relax from something that happen that day. As men get older, they go through physical changes also like women, just not as bad. They get quiet and they need a lot of alone time. You must understand that this has nothing to do with how much he loves you. He loves you enough to go to his study, man cave, or any room that he stays in to calm down and relax so he can be pleasant to everyone in the house. When I first got married, I was so in love with my husband, I wanted to be in his face 24-7, I just smothered him. As I got older, I realized that a man needs time to himself. I will never understand about a man sitting down looking at TV, every channel, never finishing one show. Just flicking through all the channels (CHANNEL SURFING). Women of God you can not change this. This Flipping Channels every few seconds is a "Man Thing". You will never be able to understand this but leave him alone in his study, man cave, or any room that he stays in a lot and let him flip channels all he wants. Do not try to sit with him in his study, man cave, or room that is his domain to look at TV. These flipping channels will drive you silly. These flipping channels calms men. In our marriage, we have a specific time every night when we look at certain shows, we both like together.

- Please keep your house clean, decorated, and beautiful so he'll be happy to come home. Put things in your house that you know he loves.
- Keep your breath and body clean, go to dentist, and GYN every six months.

- Do not sit in the back of the church and look mean. Sit in the front or near the front and smile.
- Do not carry the attitude that you do not want to be bothered with the saints.
- Do not cook in your church clothes, do not let your children wear the same clothes to church they wore all day, especially in the summer time.
- Stay out of people's houses. (I Tim 5:13, KJV)
- Learn when you are upset. Do not say nothing is wrong. Say I am upset but we will talk later. Let's forgive, go to church, and talk about it later. Do not belittle your husband and yourself by coming to the church angry and making a scene; spoil, immature children do that.
- Avoid having an inferior complex and being paranoid that everyone does not like you and is talking about you. It's a trick of the devil. God is looking at how you treat people not how they treat you anyway. Show people how saved you are. Love people like the way Jesus and Joseph did.
- Do not be in the middle of every problem in the church. Where there is smoke there is fire. Examine yourself! If you don't start anything, it won't be anything.
- Do not listen or spy on your husband's conversations. People that belong to your husband's church tell very confidential things to a Pastor that they do not want anyone to know. It is ungodly to listen. You married a Man of God, he is filled with the Holy Ghost, led by God, you trust him, and there is no need to listen or spy on the phone. A Pastor will always take phone calls at any hour. It is not your business to ask anytime, "who is that on the phone and what did they want?" Or "why you have to stay on the phone so long with that person?" It is his job.

- Do not force yourself or your ideas all the time. Do not have the attitude that if I do not do it, it will not be done or done right. No one knows everything at all times. Accept help, ideas, and advice from other people.
- Do not think you are better than anyone else, esteem others higher than yourself. (Phil 2:3, KJV)
- Do not get up and leave while your husband is preaching, do not look in your purse for long periods of time, looking down, stay in the bathroom, taking kids in bathroom excessively, and stand around the bathroom. It makes it look as if you don't want to hear your own husband preach. (People in Church really look at Apostles, Presiding Bishops, Bishops, Pastors, Prophets, Elders, Ministers, Evangelist, and Deacon Wives when they are preaching and teaching.)
- Do not break church rules; if you love God, your church and especially your husband, it is a reflection on him when you continue to break church rules.
- Do not be cruel to the saints; you will reap it.
- Do not despise small beginnings.

(Zechariah 4:10, KJV)

For who hath despised the day of small things? for they shall rejoice, and shall see the plummet in the hand of Zerubbabel with those seven; they are the eyes of the LORD, which run to and fro through the whole earth.

- Avoid charge cards, they keep you poor.
- Avoid smothering your husband, he has a job to do, love him, but do not overly cling to him. At times men of God must be alone with God.

- Do not go around your husband complaining about what you do not have or what you want when you know he can not afford it.
- Avoid leaving the church building without letting the pastor and your husband know where you are. Your husband should know where you are at all times. He should also let you know where he is at all times. It is called respecting one another.
- Avoid being jealous or insecure of anyone, especially women. Some women are not saved and come to church just to bring down the man of God. If you are doing right at home, no woman can intimidate you. Fast and pray for yourself often until you are secure in knowing that a man of God must greet, speak, shake the hand, hug, and have conferences with other women in the church. Remember, the man of God belongs to God and the people of God. He has a job he must do. A lot of times it is going to be done without you. A Man of God is something like a policeman, fireman, or a Doctor. Their wives get accustomed to interrupted Dinners, Birthdays, Special Occasions, Anniversaries, and Special Times just for the two of you. A Leader of God's people can not turn off his phone. He is on duty 24-7. Emergencies come up in their members lives such as death, hospital visits, tragic things, etc. and he must be there. A Doctor may have a "Doctor on Call". However, a Pastor who is Full Time Ministry probably will not have a "Pastor on Call" or anyone else to take his place. Take it with a smile and pray. You will get adjusted to it.
- Do not be bossy and too independent that you feel you do not need your husband.
- Do not have a sharp tongue.
- Avoid having lack of affection, love, and warmth towards your husband. Love your husband with all of your heart,

never turn your back to him and ignore him when he wants your attention. (That is a sin)

(1 Corinthians 7:3-5, KJV)

[3] Let the husband render unto the wife due benevolence: and likewise also the wife unto the husband.

[4] **The wife hath not power of her own body**, but the husband: and likewise also **the husband hath not power of his own body, but the wife.**

[5] **Defraud** ye not one the other, except it be with consent for a time, that ye may give yourselves to fasting and prayer; and come together again, that Satan tempt you not for your incontinency.

Defraud means (cheat or rob). Do not cheat or rob one another from sex, except it be with consent for a time, that ye may give yourselves to fasting and prayer.

No woman or man should be fasting all the time because they do not want to have sex.

- **Do not stay on the phone day and night listening to gossip. You have a house to clean, food to fix, clothes to wash, children to feed and make them do their school work. A holy woman must have a clean, decorated, and beautiful home that your husband will be glad to come home to! The entire house should be cleaned before he comes home and food on the table.**
- **Do not spend time at everyone's house and your house is dirty. Don't be a busybody.**
  (I Timothy 5:13, KJV) [13] And withal they learn to be idle, wandering about from house to house; and not only idle,

but tattlers also and busybodies, speaking things which they ought not.

<u>(Proverbs 25:17, KJV)</u>

Withdraw thy foot from thy neighbour's house; lest he be weary of thee, and so hate thee.

- **Do not turn your children against your husband. Do not talk bad or complain to your children about your husband. Do not talk bad or complain to your mother or family members about your husband. When you and your husband solve whatever problem you had, your mother and family will not forget and dislike your husband because what you have said. It is a sin and ungodly to do this.**

- **Do not forget your husband by only taking care of the children. Children are going to leave home mostly after they graduate, go to college, or start their new life. You will be left at home with your husband. Build a loving relationship with him now while the children are in the home so you will still know and love your husband when your children move out.**

- **Do not be lazy by always wanting to eat out. You will bankrupt your husband and your marriage if you start a habit of ordering meals. The money you spend on fast-food and restaurants would make two or three meals at home. Go through your Bank Statements from last year and add all the money you spent eating out and fast-food. It usually will be enough to pay a whole bill off. Learn from that total and do not do this. On Special Occasions eating out may be feasible.**

How can your husband preach to others, if you, your children, your house, and your attitude is not portraying what he is preaching?

Greet the Pastor and all the saints if time allows. If you are an Apostle, Assistant Pastor, Elder, Evangelist, or a Deacon's wife, all the saints may be under your husband's leadership one day and you may be the first lady. They are not going to forget how you treated them and neither will God.

Be holy around your husband and children. Live so holy that your husband will know your character and know when people lie on you. Take it from me, certain Church people will lie on you more than once. Also, learn and know your husband's character so you will know when people are lying on him. You can not control what people say or think about you; however, you can let it be a lie. Do not go around to people trying to straighten out a lie. You can live down any lie. Learn how to season your words with grace when you are upset. Just be quiet when you are upset.

We are here to be a HELP-MEET. Your job is to tell your husband what you see in people and in the church. Also, we are to warn our husband when we see the devil. We are not to dictate to him. When you share this advice please address your husband with the greatest honor, respect, and humility. Say to him, "you are the head and the man of God, the Apostle, Presiding Bishop, Bishop, Pastor, Prophet, Elder, Minister, Evangelist, or Deacon, and you would like to share something with him." Pray over it and let the Lord lead you. If he doesn't take your advice and your advice would have helped him, never tell him, "I told you so" or think he is weak or a bad leader. Your job is to pray, be sweet, and help him get out of any mess or problem he is involved in. Do not make the mistake and judge another man's servant. Do not judge your husband when he makes a mistake or because he did not listen to you. He is a Man of God, but he is not God.

(Romans 14:4, KJV)

"Who art thou that judgest another man's servant? to his own master he standeth or falleth. Yea, he shall be holden up: **for God is able to make him stand**."

God will get you! Touch not my anointed which means verbally as well.

(1 Chronicles 16:21-22, KJV)

He suffered no man to do them wrong: yea, he reproved kings for their sakes,

²² Saying, Touch not mine anointed, and do my prophets no harm.

We are favored by the Lord and we are Special Helpers. Speak to him with the right, gentle, kind, humble spirit, and share things with your husband without arguing. When he makes the wrong decision without your advice, he will see in time God has given him a GREAT GIFT, YOU! Later on, he will come to you for more advice and opinions. Even when he trusts your opinion, never debate, dictate, or think you are better than your covering. We are to commend and complement our husbands. Do not fuss over mistakes, pray, and fix it together.

I pray that this book will help you become better Apostle, Presiding Bishop, Bishop, Pastor, Prophet, Elder, Minister, Evangelist, or Deacon wives.

ELEVEN

(I Corinthians 13, Kjv)-
The Love Chapter

(I CORINTHIANS 13:3-8, KJV)

[3] And though I bestow all my goods to feed the poor, and though I give my body to be burned, and have not charity, it profiteth me nothing.

[4] Charity suffereth long, and is kind; charity envieth not; charity vaunteth not itself, is not puffed up,

[5] Doth not behave itself unseemly, seeketh not her own, is not easily provoked, thinketh no evil;

[6] Rejoiceth not in iniquity, but rejoiceth in the truth;

[7] Beareth all things, believeth all things, hopeth all things, endureth all things.

[8] Charity never faileth: but whether there be prophecies, they shall fail; whether there be tongues, they shall cease; whether there be knowledge, it shall vanish away.

Women of God you were already taught the Love Chapter in the Bible. (I Corinthians 13, KJV). No matter what good deeds you do in the church and life, and have not charity in your home with your husband, it profits nothing. You can preach the paint off a Church Wall and do not have charity in your home with your husband. Your preaching is in vain. Charity begins at home with your husband

and children. Charity suffered long. We had a very small church; however, my husband preached at many different churches. I suffered greatly from many different people that were in the Church World. Everyone that goes to church is not always sweetly saved or saved. They could not touch my husband because he was so anointed and powerful, they were afraid. So, they persecuted me. I can hardly believe what I am about to tell you, but all of that suffering made me cry a lot, fast, pray, seek God's face, and made me the Woman in Zion I am today! Suffering and heartbreak give you a great anointing with God! We are to be kind to everyone and especially to our husband and church members. Love your husband like the Bible says. Charity vaunt not itself. Vaunt means go around boasting excessively about what you have or acting superior to everyone else because you are an Apostle, Presiding Bishop, Bishop, Pastor, Prophet, Elder, Minister, Evangelist or Deacon's wife. Charity will never have envy in your heart. Envy is a feeling of discontent and resentful longing aroused by someone else's possessions, qualities, or blessings. When you are in the Church World there will always be people that have more possessions, qualities, or blessings than you. If you do not feel glad for them it is time for you to pray and fast it out of you. You can not be a good saint or Clergy's Wife with envy, jealousy, or covetousness in your heart. You as a woman of God can not go around your house or the house of God being puffed-up because you did not get your way. Being the Clergy's wife does not mean you can have it your way. The longer you are a Clergy wife you will be humble enough to accept many things that will not go your way in your home and in the House of God. It is all about pleasing God. Your husband, the Chosen One does not seek to please you, but God. It is all about serving God and staying in His will. As a woman of God with your important position, you can not afford to behave unseemly, especially with your husband and the members of the Church. Charity seeketh not her own. You can not be selfish and overbearing with any of your gifts. You will want to give other people a chance to use their gifts. It can not be all about you. I have to lead the choir; I have to be the president of the all the auxiliaries. Your husband is not going to put you over everything in the Church because you are his wife. He is led by Our Savior, not you! This is kingdom work. Charity is not easily provoked. You have the Holy Ghost and you will need the Holy Ghost dealing with people in the Church World. You will need to fast and pray a lot. In the Church World, people will try to provoke you, stir you up, and try to get you to rise up and sin because you let them provoke you. Again, I want to remind you that everyone that attend Church is not sweetly saved or saved. They will try very hard to get a rise out of you, to get an unfavorable emotion or reaction from you. Do not do it just pray. Do not sit around your house or the House of God thinking evil. It is easy to think evil about people that try to hurt you. Do not do it just pray and fast it out. Do not rejoice when someone falls or God punish someone for hurting you or your husband. They have a soul and we are all about saving souls. Rejoice in the truth.

Charity beareth all things, believeth all things, hopeth all things, and endureth all things. As a woman of God married to a Clergy Man, you will have to bear and endure things that you never thought you had to bear. When my husband first started his church, he was so hard on me. He was harder on me than anyone. I thought it was so unfair. If I did something wrong in front of the church, like lay someone out. I was young only 19 years old. I had to go before the whole church and ask for forgiveness. Sometimes it would hurt me so bad, I would be crying and apologizing. This open rebuke helped me a lot. God knew I never wanted to do anything wrong in his house or my house. I want to go back with God. Therefore, I started seasoning my words with grace and be very careful not to offend someone or I would back in front of the church apologizing. I fasted and prayed so much not to do anything wrong. I became an expert at holding my peace and letting God fight my battles. I did not get away with anything in my husband's church. If my husband called me by my first name and said "Judith I need to talk to you". Lord, I knew I had done something wrong and he was going discuss it with me. My husband had a way about him that when he was teaching, correcting, and instructing you, he never raised his voice. He would be so sweet chastising you; you would feel so bad. You would never be found in that position again. One time I had saved up for this beautiful robe. First time ever buying robes from a professional robe store. One of the members came crying that she did not have money to get her robe. My husband gave her my brand-new robe. I could not believe he did that. I bared it and endured so many similar things. I did not understand why he was so hard on me for years.

One of my jobs was to make sure all services start on time. I could not be late. My husband taught me to start the service on time if no one was there except you and Jesus. So, I was a Sunday School Teacher, President of the Annual Women's Week service, and President of the Women's Department. Being the head of the Women's Department and President of the Annual Women's Week was the hardest job ever. Trying to get women of all ages to work for the Kingdom of God and turn in money to help build the work of the Lord. These two jobs made me cry many nights. The disappointments of women not coming to these services, not working at all, and plenty of other heartaches that I kept to myself. I really learned how to cry to God until our Annual Women's Week became the largest service of the year and the women raised more money than churches much larger than ours. They turned my tears, crying, heartaches into joy. All the women of our Church attended Annual Women's Week unless there were Extenuating Circumstances. We have some awesome women of God at our church. They would sell candy, Mother's Day, and Valentine baskets, cakes, and dinners to come up their goal. During the Covid-19 Pandemic, one of our women hand-made the prettiest face masks! She sold so many and turned the money over to our Annual Women's Day. Another one just asked all of her friends and relatives for a love offering for her pastor and turned in about $500.00. They are such a beautiful group of women that are faithful to the Lord and the ministry. I would have never experienced their greatness if I stopped when I was crying. My husband told me you are an Evangelist and you should be able to stand anything. He did not mentor a weak woman. All that hardness made me strong and the woman of Zion that I am today. One Sunday my husband told the whole church that God had prepared me to be Asst. Pastor of the Church. I was stunned. I could not speak, I wanted to decline the position but I just was so shocked that I could not speak. After this, my husband told me that he was being extra hard on me because I was going to hold the second highest position in the Church and he wanted me to be strong in the Lord and do a good job in my new position.

You have to learn right now that you will not understand all people in the Church World. The more you do for some people in the Church World, the worst they will act towards you sometimes. After helping them save their house, pay bills for them, and come to their rescue, they will leave your church and they will talk about you like a dog. Take all this to God, never, try to go to people in the Church World or church members that left your church to straighten up a lie they told on you. Pray and live the lie down. Let God take care of it. Never go to Church members that have left your church unless God leads you to do so. If you beg them to come back to your church, if they come back when their heart is not there, you are going to suffer greatly. Therefore, love them and let them go! You must believe all things, every promise that the Bible and God says, no matter how long it takes. You have to have Hope in the Lord to survive living a Clergy Wife life. With God, all things are possible.

TWELVE

Husbands (God's Rule For You By Scriptures)

(Genesis 2:18, KJV)

¹⁸ And the LORD God said, It is not good that the man should be alone; I will make him an help meet for him.

And the Lord God said, "It is not good that the man should be alone; I will make him an help meet for him. **(Genesis 2:18, KJV).** He will give you someone that will be just right for you and meet all of his needs and they will be one flesh. Things are better when you have a wife by your side. I told my husband when we almost lost every material thing, not to worry, if he sinks, I will be right there with him to help him rise again.

(Genesis 2:24, KJV)

Therefore a man shall leave his father and his mother and hold fast to his wife, and they shall become one flesh.

A real Man of God will leave his father and his mother and get an apartment or house for his wife. He will hold fast to his wife. He will put his wife first, not be a momma's boy, without checking everything with his momma about what to do in his house.

(Deuteronomy 24:5, KJV)

"When a man is newly married, he shall not go out with the army or be liable for any other public duty. He shall be free at home <u>one year to be happy</u> with his wife whom he has taken.

(Proverbs 5:18-19, KJV)

Let your fountain be blessed, and rejoice in the wife of your youth, a lovely deer, a graceful doe. Let her breasts fill you at all times with delight; be intoxicated always in her love.

Enjoy being with your wife you married in your youth. Have as many as children that Our Savior will allow. Continue to cherish, love, adore, appreciate, treasure, and value her when she grows old. Only be satisfied with only her. Be intoxicated with your wife all through your marriage. Have affairs with your own wife. Do not get bored with her. Always put the excitement in your marriage. If you let God lead you, this love and affection will grow stronger and deeper as the years go by. She is the one that the Lord gave you. Continue to enjoy and get delight only from her! The more love and care you give her she will multiply it.

(Proverbs 12:4, KJV)

An excellent wife is the crown of her husband, but she who brings shame is like rottenness in his bones.

Your wife is the crown to her husband and he will treat her as a Queen.

(Proverbs 18:22, KJV)

He who finds a wife finds a good thing and obtains favor from the Lord.

All good and perfect gifts come from above. When you find your good wife, realize it is God that obtained her for you, not your own will. God gave you this precious gift by God's good providence towards you.

(Ecclesiastes 9:9, KJV)

Enjoy life with the wife whom you love, all the days of your vain life that he has given you under the sun, because that is your portion in life and in your toil at which you toil under the sun.

A Man in ministry knows he cannot be in Church Work 100% of the time and forget the duties that are listed in the Word of God to love his wife. Enjoy your life with your wife, not just when you become newlyweds, but your entire marriage.

(Ecclesiasticus 26:3, KJV)

"A good wife is a good portion, which shall be given in the portion of them that fear the Lord."

Your Wife is your portion, a great part of your life and a piece of you. Therefore, when you work extremely hard on a secular job or for the Kingdom. You must take the time with your wife regardless of how busy and anointed you are, enjoy life with your wife! Don't be so righteous, holy, and anointed that you are no good being a GOOD HUSBAND. You have to spend time going fun places other than church, church conventions, and prayer meetings. Enjoy life with your wife at restaurants, hotels, time shares, holidays, cruises, parks, museums, amusement parks, and places that you went to before you got married. The romance must continue or you will be just roommates. We've been married for forty-seven years and we continue date and spend the time to have fun with each other.

(Matthew 19:4-6, KJV)

⁴ And he answered and said unto them, Have ye not read, that he which made them at the beginning made them male and female,

⁵ And said, For this cause shall a man leave father and mother, and shall cleave to his wife: and they twain shall be one flesh?

⁶ Wherefore they are no more twain, but one flesh. What therefore God hath joined together, let not man put asunder.

God is repeating Himself again. That means it is very, very, important for a Man in ministry to leave his parents, and cleave to his wife. Leave your parent's house and move in an apartment or home with your wife.

(Romans 12:9, KJV) "*Let* love be without dissimulation (pretense). Abhor that which is evil; **cleave to that which is good.**"

Cleave to your wife because she is good. You are to stick to, to adhere; to hold to, to unite, to fit, to be united closely in interest, and affections to your wife. Cleave to Jehovah, your God. (**Josh. 23, KJV**) After cleaving to Jehovah your God. Our Savior wants you to cleave to your wife. God has given her to you. **Be happy to be with your wife**, you are two people but God has made you one flesh. The Lord has joined you together to be husband and wife let no man put you asunder. Let no man put you apart, separate, or divide you. Not your mother, father, best friend, or anyone.

(John 3:16-17, KJV)

¹⁶ For God so loved the world, that he gave his only begotten Son, that whosoever believeth in him should not perish, but have everlasting life.

¹⁷ For God sent not his Son into the world to condemn the world; but that the world through him might be saved.

"For God so loved the world, that he gave his only Son, that whoever believes in Him should not perish, but have eternal life. (**John 3:16 KJV**) For God did not send his Son into the world to condemn the world, but in order that the world might be saved through him. We are living for eternal life and the love must start between husband and wife. For God is love and he wants us to love one another and be happily married.

(**John 14:15, KJV**)

"If you love me, you will keep my commandments.

If you and your wife really Love the Lord, you will keep all of His commandments. God commanded us to love one another starting with husband and wife. If you want to see Jesus you must discipline your marriage like the Bible says.

(**Romans 7:2, KJV**)

² For the woman which hath an husband is bound by the law to her husband so long as he liveth; but if the husband be dead, she is loosed from the law of her husband.

The woman is bound by God's Law to her husband while he lives, but if he dies, she is released from the law of marriage. When we first get married, do not look at marriage as a person buying a car. If I do not want or like the car anymore, I will take it back. My husband said, "God ordained us to be married. We sought the Lord for knowledge to make our marriage happy and last until one of us die." Both of your minds have to be made up to make your marriage happy and last. Don't seek to be loosed from your wife. I have met people that stayed married for one month and got a divorce. I told the young man you did not even give yourself time to know your wife. The first year you are just getting to know one another.

(Deuteronomy 24:5, KJV)

"When a man is newly married, he shall not go out with the army or be liable for any other public duty. He shall be free at home one year to be happy with his wife whom he has taken.

You can date for thousands of years but you do not know anyone until you say "I do and live with them". The first year you find out what each other do not like. It is easy after you find out what things get on your nerve. Just make up in both of your minds, we are not going to get on one another's nerve. Just stop doing things that make one another upset. After about a year, you will know everything that each of you don't like and work to stop doing those things. When you love the Lord and want to please Him, you will surrender your will and your way. You will seek to please God by surrendering little or big things that upset one another. Everyone is reared in a different house, by different parents, and have difference ways. With love you can conquer all differences and live happy together for a life time.

(Romans 13:1, KJV)

Let every soul be subject unto the higher powers. For there is no power but of God: the powers that be are ordained of God.

Let every person be subject to the higher power and that is God. He has all authorities. For there is no power or authority except from the Lord, and those that exist have been instituted by God. Your marriage has been instituted by Our Savior and He does not make any mistakes. God has authority over the husband and the husband has authority over the wife. Both of you are to be subject to God's Holy Word.

(1 Corinthians 6:18, KJV)

[18] Flee fornication. Every sin that a man doeth is without the body; but he that committeth fornication sinneth against his own body.

Man of God you are filled with the Holy Ghost and you will not let fornication once be named about you. You will flee from sexual immorality. Every other sin a person commits is outside the body, but the sexually immoral person sins against his own body.

(1 Corinthians 11:8, KJV)

[8] For the man is not of the woman: but the woman of the man.

If you love your wife like you love your own body, her desire will be to you. The woman came from your rib, so you can walk along side of her and be complete with your rib. She was created for you from God.

(1 Corinthians 7:1-5, KJV)

[1] Now concerning the things whereof ye wrote unto me: It is good for a man not to touch a woman.

[2] Nevertheless, to avoid fornication, let every man have his own wife, and let every woman have her own husband.

[3] Let the husband render unto the wife due benevolence: and likewise also the wife unto the husband.

[4] The wife hath not power of her own body, but the husband: and likewise also the husband hath not power of his own body, but the wife.

[5] Defraud ye not one the other, except it be with consent for a time, that ye may give yourselves to fasting and prayer; and come together again, that Satan tempt you not for your incontinency.

When you are saved it is not good for a man to touch a woman. The flesh is weaker than you think, do not tempt the flesh. So, to avoid fornication, let every man have his own wife, and let every woman have her own husband. Let the husband render (give, provide, furnish and make available) the wife due benevolence such as love, kindness, gentleness, goodness, and yes SEX. No husband or wife should stop having sex unless they are fasting before God and each of them have agreed to that fast. The fast should only be for a short time so you can fulfill one another's sexual needs. Do not break up your own marriage because you fast and pray all the time. This kind of behavior will cause a good husband to turn to other woman for the sex that his wife would not give him. Also, this kind of behavior will cause a good wife to turn to other men for the sex that her husband would not give her. First of all, if you do not like sex you should not get married in the first place. Give your whole life over to God and God's work. Whether you like sex or not you can not deny sex with your husband or wife. Talk to each other about this and solve this problem. If you can not solve it between each other try going to talk to a GYN doctor, PCP, a Christian Sex Counselor, Marriage Counselor, and Our Savior to solve this problem. Find out if this is a physical problem or something else. You must find out the problem and solve it.

My husband still teaches Young Pastors to make sure they do not get so busy with God's work that they forget they have a wife. She has needs just like a man. Often young pastors get so zealous with

God and His work they neglect time with their wife. No married woman should feel single with a husband lying right beside her in bed. Young Pastors can be so zealous about ministry that they spend all their spare time at church, neglecting their wife and family. This is not right. God is expecting you to put him first, but not neglect your duties to your wife. Young Pastors have to be taught how to do this. Many young Pastors are separated or have divorced their wives the first year because of this. It is not the Lord's will to break up marriages. Marriage is honorable and the bed is not defile. Ladies please let your husband read this if he is doing this. A pastor can be overworked. This happens when a pastor has a small poor church. Also, it can happen to any Young Pastor over a small or large congregation. No pastor can do it all. You just do your best and let God do the rest. Do not punish your wife by ignoring her. Not spending time with her and not having sex. The husband should give to his wife her conjugal rights, and likewise the wife to her husband. For the wife does not have authority over her own body, but the husband does. Likewise, the husband does not have authority over his own body, but the wife does. Do not deprive one another, except perhaps by agreement for a limited time, that you may devote yourselves to fasting; but then come together again, so that Satan may not tempt you because of your lack of sex.

God wants you to put him first and let your wife be next. Your bodies belong to each other, and you can not be so overly engaged in church work until you are too tired to date, spend time, and be romantic with your wife. Sex is her conjugal right. This is grounds by law to get a divorce. Young Pastors and Bishops please take this seriously!

This is repeated for the Husbands.

My husband and I took the time to date each other. When we first got married, he could not afford a box of expensive candy or a dozen of roses. Instead he would bring me my favorite candy bar, a big Snicker Bar, and One rose from 7-Eleven. I was in love with this man so, I was overjoyed because he was thinking about me. We would keep a blanket in the trunk of our car. We went to the park, laid down on the blanket, talked, laughed, and enjoyed one another for free! The more you spend time together, the more your love grows. Many married couples are so busy raising their kids they forget about romance. Consequently, after your kids leave home, you won't know one another and you'll get a divorce if you don't change. Many married couples were together for twenty, thirty, and forty years and were divorced because of this. Never stop loving one another and going on dates! It doesn't matter how many children you have. For a few years I raised seven children, took care my mom, my mother in law, and church mother. They were all senior citizens and needed a lot of assistance. My husband would hire a saved, seasoned mother in church to watch everyone for a week or for a weekend for our vacations.

When my husband started working for the government while Pastoring a Church, we continued to do things that newlyweds do. We loved dressing up in Formal Attire and going to expensive restaurants. We would go to hotels, restaurants, cruises, time shares and people would think we just got married. Time shares are a blessing because you can stay at beautiful, romantic places for a week for the price of one night at a hotel. Time Shares ran bonus weeks most the time. I have been married to this wonderful Man of God for forty-seven years and we vacationed a whole week at time shares for all my birthdays, our Anniversaries, Thanksgiving, and Christmas. Also, we will take a week off when we worked really hard in church; for example, big special services like Church Women's Week, Pastor's and Church Anniversaries. When we first got married, my husband did not see the need for all these vacations, he did it to keep me happy. I spent a lot of time crying; I was 19-year-old when he became a Pastor. I felt that I could bear all the frustration that people put on me if I could just get away for a week with my husband. I lived for vacations and still love them! Vacations with my husband was my city of refuge. In our later years of marriage, my husband told me he took me to these vacations for my sake to make me happy. However, he told me he needed to get away and just did not realize it. He looks forward to resting his mind and body during our great get-a-ways.

Pastors or any Leaders should not talk to any women in your study alone. I am not jealous of any woman on the planet. Pastors and Bishops have been lied on about trying to seduce women. Therefore, keep your pastor's door open or let your wife sit in your conference. When you have conference with a woman always have a nice big desk between you and her. Also, never talk to a woman member about her lack of sex life with her husband. Turn her over to the elderly consecrated mother of the church, a Marriage Counselor, or the wife of the Pastor that can keep secrets.

(Ephesians 4:30, KJV)

And do not grieve the Holy Spirit of God, by whom you were sealed for the day of redemption.

Do not grieve the Holy Spirit of God by letting corrupt communication proceed out of your mouth, or being bitter, mean, and unreasonable towards your wife. Do not fuss, yell, argue with your wife. If you are a Man of God, you will love, provide food, and other things necessary for growth, health, and well-being for your wife and family. A Leader will sustain, and maintain his wife and family. Chosen Men of God do not yell, scream, slap, push, shove, hit, punch, or do any harm physically, emotionally, or mentally to their wives. This kind of behavior will grieve the Lord. Please do not nag your wife to death by telling her "I am the head of the house" and you have to do what I say! Just be the head and do what the scriptures demonstrate and explain how to be the Head of the

House. Your actions speak louder than your words. If you love your wife like you love yourself, she will have no problem obeying and honoring you. When you have a problem, sit down like two adults and discuss it. My husband and I look at our marriage as a Company. He is the CEO and I am the Asst. CEO. In a company when there is a problem, you do not scream, yell, shout, and find fault in one another about the problem. You sit down calmly like two mature adults and find out what the problem is and how to solve it. Do what is BEST for the Business and the Business is BEING HAPPILY MARRIED according to the WORD.

(Ephesians 5:1-5, 17 & 18, KJV)

1 Be ye therefore followers of God, as dear children;

2 And walk in love, as Christ also hath loved us, and hath given himself for us an offering and a sacrifice to God for a sweetsmelling savour.

3 But fornication and all uncleanness, or covetousness, let it not be once named among you, as becometh saints;

4 Neither filthiness, nor foolish talking, nor jesting, which are not convenient: but rather giving of thanks

5 For this ye know, that no whoremonger, nor unclean person, nor covetous man, who is an idolater, hath any inheritance in the kingdom of Christ and of God.

17 Wherefore be ye not unwise, but understanding what the will of the Lord is.

18 And be not drunk with wine, wherein is excess; but be filled with the Spirit.

Therefore, be imitators of God, as beloved children; walk in love, as Christ loved us and gave himself for us, a fragrant offering and sacrifice to God. Sexual immorality and all impurity or covetousness must not even be named among you as is proper among saints. Let there be no filthiness nor foolish talk nor crude joking, which are out of place, but instead let there be thanksgiving. For you may be sure of this, that everyone who is sexually immoral or impure or who is covetous (that is, an idolater), has no inheritance in the kingdom of Christ and God.

When you are a real Man of God and an excellent husband, you will imitate God by loving your wife like God loves His church. That is unconditional LOVE. Whatever you have to do to show your wife that you love her unconditional like God. You will love her so much until she knows without a shadow of doubt, that you love her, you adore her and your family. You will take the time out to know her and understand her better than she understands herself. When I got married, I was a little, nineteen-year-old girl that was spoiled and had to grow up. My husband was a real man and spiritual enough to help me grow up naturally and spiritually. His wisdom helped me mature into another level in God.

He was poor when I first married him, yet he was so rich in God with wisdom and unconditional love for me. I knew he came from God. I would drive around and cry like a baby because God gave me my husband. I loved him from the first time we ate together at a Chinese Restaurant in Baltimore, Maryland. I did not know what was wrong with me yet everyone else knew. He made me laugh, smile, and feel so good inside like no other human being. One encounter with him changed me for life. He brought the best out of me when I was with him. Through his letters or a telephone call, he encouraged me to be better, happier, and he inspired me to be the best I could possibly be on this earth. My husband still inspires me after forty-seven years of marriage. His unconditional love for my daughter and me has been heavenly right here on Earth. The love he allowed us to see, feel, and share between us protected and covered us both from all the evils, hates, dislikes, disapprovals, and the emps that the devil has sent our way. His precious love has been enough. It was never a joke when people asked me how I was doing, I would say" I got Jesus and John and that is enough".

A Christian Man will walk in love always as Christ loved us and gave himself for us, starting in his home, with his wife, and children. He will walk in love always as Christ. He will give himself to his wife and family. He will give up a lot of luxuries and make sacrifices for his wife and family. I have had so many sicknesses and diseases but my husband made sure I had the best insurance which cost him over one thousand dollars a month. It was so high because I had preexisting conditions. He did it and also gave my daughter the best insurance. Yet, he did not have insurance for himself. When he went to the doctor they asked "What kind of insurance do you have?" my husband said, "Self-Insurance" the young lady did not know what that meant; therefore, an older and more experience nurse said, "That means he does not have any insurance and pays for it himself. My husband always made sure that my daughter and I have the best before he bought anything for himself. He made sure I always had a good running car. One time my car had a flat tire or broke down on the way to work. The next day I went to work with a new car. My co-workers told me people do not buy a new car because it had a flat tire or broke down once. I told them my husband traveled a lot during revivals and he wanted me to have a safe car. He bought me a new car because he would not have to worry about my car breaking down when he was away.

A real saved Man will be led by the Holy Ghost and will not get caught up in any sexual impurity or covetousness. Most of my married life, I weighed three hundred and twenty-five pounds (325 lbs.). My husband worked clerical positions, then advanced as a computer operator on the government base. He worked for seventeen years around all types of women that were blonds, red heads, and had cute model types. I was never jealous because my husband carried himself in a Holy way at all times and he was filled with the Holy Ghost. My husband lived such a spotless life, he helped to get me a job on the government base. After working there for a while, a black man asked me how in the world did my husband get a job working with all those women. I told him because no one had to worry about him sexually harassing any of those women. The women and those in authority knew what kind of man they hired. He's a saved man with integrity, strong moral principles, uprightness, honesty, and honor. He never was filthy, foolish talking, or entertained crude joking. My husband was always carried himself in a proper manner according to the Word. A Chosen Man of God is always thinking about Heaven. He lives to have inheritance in the kingdom of God.

A Holy Man is very wise and knows how to conduct himself at all times. He knows he is the head of the house and that it is God's will for him to have a peaceful, happy marriage, and a family life filled with love. A Leader knows he must always get more understanding from God and will always seek the Lord and be filled with the Spirit of the Holy Ghost.

(Ephesians 5:21, 23-33, KJV)

[23] For the **husband is the head of the wife**, even as Christ is the head of the church: and he is the saviour of the body.

[24] Therefore as the church is subject unto Christ, so let the wives be to their own husbands in every thing.

[25] **Husbands, love your wives**, even as Christ also loved the church, and gave himself for it;

²⁶ That he might sanctify and cleanse it with the washing of water by the word,

²⁷ That he might present it to himself a glorious church, not having spot, or wrinkle, or any such thing; but that it should be holy and without blemish.

²⁸ **So ought men to love their wives as their own bodies**. He that loveth his wife loveth himself.

²⁹ For no man ever yet hated his own flesh; but nourisheth and cherisheth it, even as the Lord the church:

³⁰ For we are members of his body, of his flesh, and of his bones.

³¹ For this cause shall a man leave his father and mother, and shall be joined unto his wife, and they two shall be one flesh.

³² This is a great mystery: but I speak concerning Christ and the church.

³³ Nevertheless let every one of you in particular so love his wife even as himself; and the wife see that she reverence her husband.

1. A Leader will take a stand as the head of the wife as Christ is the head of the church. He is a strong Holy man that leads his wife and family while communicating with God. The man is an example of Christ in character, thought, emotion, and deeds. He leads by honoring the Lord in dealing with his plans to manage his life and family. He leads the way in honoring God, keeping prayer, fasting, and reading of the Word with his family. The head of the household teaches his family how important it is to be saved and shows his family how important it is to be in church. He does not send them

the church, but leads them to church. Our Savior teaches him how to have necessary conversations with his wife and family. He knows how God loves quality time with his creation, therefore, he will always observe his wife and family to see when he must have quality time with them. Having wonderful communication with your wife and family is the glue that holds love and happiness in your home. The husband is the leader because he can tell when something is not right with his household. He will have a compassionate way to address the root of the problem by talking it out. The Man of God, which is the head of the house will always be the first to make sacrifices for his family. The **husband** must work closely with his wife to provide emotional and financial support for the children. The leader will provide appropriate monitoring, discipline, and most importantly, remain a permanent and loving presence in his family's life.

2. The Head of the house is open to get advice from his wife about his strengths and weaknesses without getting upset. It will improve their marriage and family. He is able to communicate to his wife and family about their strengths and weaknesses without verbal abuse. A Godly husband will always encourage the wife and family to do good, acceptable, and perfect will of God when they get off track. The Leader has Holy standards and takes the lead to help his wife and family make it to Heaven. He is always content with what the Lord has allowed him to have and teaching his family contentment. He sets the attitude and feelings about what is happening in their lives. He makes his home a positive environment to encourage, give support, confidence, hope, uplift, inspire, and motivate his family about life. He teaches his family how to love and sacrifice for one another. He guides each member of the household to discover, develop, and deploy their unique gifts in God's service.

3. As the Head of the House, it is your responsibility to see that you have all the characteristics of **(Galatians 5:22-23, KJV)** in your heart and also in your wife and family. The" FRUIT OF THE SPIRIT". You, your wife, and family must have love, joy, peace, longsuffering, gentleness, goodness, faith, meekness, and temperance which is self-control. These qualities are vital for a healthy marriage and family. You take the lead and they will follow. Whatever you give your wife she will multiply it. If you are mean, yell, scream, bitter towards her, she will multiply it back to you. You can not beat a woman being wicked, mean, bitter, and hateful. Be sweet towards her with love and understanding that God is going to give you. If you are patient, loving, and have all the characteristics of **(Galatians 5:22-23, KJV),** she will multiply the love and kindness you show her. Most normal, saved women or any normal woman will imitate what you show her. If you have Holy attributes flowing from you, it will overtake your wife and family and they will seek to be like you. The Head of the House is an example of Christ Jesus living through you.

4. Sometimes the leader has to sanctify and cleanse his wife and family with the Word of God. When you disagree with the family, tell them why by using the Word of God. The Word will get your wife and family back on track. You can not let your wife or your family do things that are UNGODLY in your home or car. If you do not drink, smoke, do drugs, yell, scream, do not allow them to do these things in your home, even if they may not be saved. Do not allow your unsaved children to bring boys or girls in your house and shut their doors and have sex in your Holy Home. This is your HOME, they do not pay any bills and give any money to the living expenses, so do not allow it. When they are over 18 years old living in your home, do not allow them to bring sin into your home. You are still the Head of The House. My husband only

raised his voice once in forty-seven years, that was when I was nineteen years old. He speaks to me, children, and church members with authority not by yelling and screaming. My husband had the ability to set the house in order in such a sweet way with his God Given Authority. My daughter and I learned that when Daddy said NO, it is NO, it will never change. We still have respect for him as the leader of the House. Your wife and children will respect you for standing up for Godly principles. Children expect parents to tell them the truth at all times and they will respect and love you for it.

5. As the Head of the House, it is your job to seek the Lord at all times to help your family to strive to live without a spot, wrinkle, or any such thing. The goal for your wife and family is to be holy and without blemish. It is an enormous task but you can do it with the love, wisdom, understanding, and help of the Holy Ghost.

6. Again, it is very, very, very imperative when God repeats the same thing in one chapter in the Bible. God repeatly tells the Husband that he ought to LOVE THEIR WIVES as their own body. When the Head of the House loves his wife as his own body, he will nourish and cherish her, even as Christ Loves, Nourishes, and Cherishes the Church. The Man of God will love and provide food and all substances necessary for growth, health, and well-being. The leader will sustain and maintain his wife and family. Husbands do not yell, scream, slap, push, shove, hit, punch or do any harm physically, emotionally or mentally to their wives. My ordained husband has never belittled me, called me out my name, never called me dumb or stupid. There were many things I did not know, but he never called me dumb.

   a. He explained how he wanted me to take care of our house hold bills and do business. Now I am an expert in Business.

b. I did not want to learn, but he kept telling me that if he got sick or died, I needed to know these things.

Since I've been married, I have seen a few women lose their husbands by death and did not know how to write a check, did not know how to do business. I heard a woman that always said, "My husband will take care of everything." Yes, her husband took care of everything, but when he died, she found out that he had left her out the will and left everything to someone else. Some of these women have had nervous breakdowns, heart attacks, never recovered from it; some have died. A real husband and man of God would never deceive his wife like that. My husband would always let me know about house documents and business transactions. He never hid anything from me because he respected his HELPMEET.

(I JOHN 3:7, KJV): Little children, let no man deceive you: he that doeth righteousness is righteous, even as he is righteous. A RIGHTEOUS HUSBND PRACTICE RIGHTEOUSNESS.

I have been married forty-seven years and He has never yelled, screamed, slapped, pushed, shoved, hit, or punched me. He has never caused any physical, mental, or emotional harm. Remember, I just turned nineteen years old when I first married my husband, I was saved, spoiled, and did a lot of silly things to get my way. Any other man would have knocked me clean out. However, he would tell me what is right, pray for me, and do something nice for me! Eventually I got sick of my own self and ashamed of the way I was treating an excellent husband. I was extremely tired of acting immature and asked God to help me be more like Him. Through much fasting and praying, I became the most obedient, sweet, kind, and submissive wife. I was and still is. I would tell people, I felt like I could get the HEAVEN just on MY OBEDIENCE TO MY HUSBAND.

7. Whether unsaved or saved people look at your marriage, they should see the Love of God. They should see how Christians love their spouse and family as Christ loves the Church. Marriage should be a Christian fellowship and friendship; deeper than any love on the planet. Throughout our marriage people have seen us on cruises, parks, restaurants, and other places and they would say "Are you Married?". We would reply, "yes!" They would be shocked how long we've been married because we have always resembled newlyweds. One time we were early for my daughter's orientation at school; we sat and talked and had a great time just talking. A woman came and asked us "Are you married?" We said, "Yes, happily married for years. She said, "You are really married? You are talking to one another!" She said her husband never talks to her. We used that opportunity to tell people when you are saved and God put you together, this is how to love and act towards one another. One time we were at a seafood restaurant and I was cracking my husband's lobster legs and putting the meat into his mouth. A woman came over and said "Are you married? I said, "Yes". She said, "You are making me look really bad in front of my husband. I told her that my husband was from North Carolina and he did not start eating seafood until I married him. I told her I have been cracking his shells and putting it in his mouth for Forty-seven years. I am happy to do it. My husband has been such a Wonderful Man of God and husband until I spoil him. I love doing things for him. He has never put butter or jelly on his bread, I do it. I sit him

down and prepare his food and serve his food like he is in a five-star expensive restaurant. I love spoiling him because he is worthy of it. When I was young and foolish, he prayed and treated me like a Queen anyway. I love treating him like a King, because he is worthy of it. It is the Head of the House duty to make sure his family life flows like a river and a river never stop flowing. You and your husband both share responsibilities to make your marriage work. No husband should be saying, "I am the Head of this House and you will obey me". When you are really the Head of the House you never have to say it out loud because when you do as you suppose to do as the Head of the House, you do not have to tell your wife or family that you are the Head of the House, you just be the Head of the House.

8. Previously, I was physically ill and I could not take care of myself many times in my marriage. I could not walk and because of excruciating pain, I wished for death. My husband encouraged me all the time and said "Don't get discouraged, God is going to Heal you." I loved how he prayed for me all the time, even now he prays for me around three times a day. I was sick on many occasions, he brought groceries, washed and put away the dishes, swept and mopped the floors. He did the cleaning of the house, the laundry, took me to the hospitals, doctors, lab, and etc. At first, he would buy fast-food. I was so sick of fast food, but I would not say anything. He never cooked and did not know how to cook because I was and still is a **(Titus 2 and a Proverbs 31, KJV)** wife. I did all the grocery shopping, cooking, and all house wife duties before I got sick. One day he carried me into the kitchen, sat me down, and asked me how to cook (baked chicken, string beans, and potatoes). He did a wonderful job and my heart almost burst wide open from happiness. He never told people that I was that sick. My husband was doing everything that a wife supposed to do. He knew I

loved going to church, but I did not want people to see me in my poor condition of not being able to walk. Therefore, my sweet Head of the House would wash me up, dry me off, wash my hair, fix my hair, and put my clothes on me. I never knew a man would love me like this and be so gentle and kind. He would take me to the church early so no one could see I could not walk, and wait until everyone left to take me home. When he did this, I fell more deeply in love with him. The way my Head of the House has treated me down through the years causes me to do anything for him. When my body was sick at different times, he always took good and excellent care of me. He is always glad to help me with a Smile. Therefore, at certain times in your marriage, you can not be concerned about gender roles. He did all those things a wife would do; however, it did not take away from him being the Head of the House. As the Leader, you do what is necessary for your company and team. Your company is your marriage managed by you and your wife.

9. I love him to the moon and back. God is the center of our marriage. I feel that we are breathing from the same lung and our hearts are beating from one heart.

10. For this cause shall a man leave his father and mother, and shall be joined unto his wife, and they two shall be one flesh. You and your wife are joined together as one flesh, physically, mentally, and emotionally. She is your first concern. You must have a budget for all income and expenses. The both of you must sit down and figure out your monthly income and plan your monthly spending. My husband is the Head of our House, always has been, yet we made an agreement never to buy anything expensive without sitting down and talking about it. He is the Leader but every time he wanted to get a new car, new house, new furniture, we discussed it. He showed me respect and I reciprocated it. If I wanted something and it did not go with the budget, he would say

no, not now, maybe later when our finances get better. I would accept that without fussing. He could say NO in such a wonderful, calm way.

11. We would compete during the year to see which one of us could raise the most money to pay off bills by Christmas time. Christmas is a time my husband takes off work, and shut the Church down for one week to be with his wife and family. He would tell the members at his Church to enjoy their family. He would advise the men to make sure they did not sit in front of the TV for a week but spend quality time with their wife and family. We taught our children the real meaning of Christmas and would read the Christmas passage from the Bible every Christmas. We taught them the season is about Jesus and giving. We gave each of our children reasonable gifts but the Greatest Gift was giving to one another; taking time to love, play, and enjoy one another. He was a Pastor yet he would crawl around the house giving our kids a horsey ride on his back, fill the room with balloons, and everyone would play. Our home consisted of my husband and me, all the children, my mother, his mother, and the mother of our church. The three mothers were senior citizens in their seventies and we all had fun. We would all get in our fifteen-passenger van and go to the Christmas lights in different neighborhoods. Our family went to Virginia Beach, Newport News, Children museums, Planetarium, Norfolk Zoo, Virginia Air & Space Science Center, Portsmouth Naval Shipyard Museum, library, the park, and other family entertainment places.

12. **(EPESIAN 5:32, KJV)**

[32] This is a great mystery: but I speak concerning Christ and the church.

To the world this is a great mystery, that a man can love his wife for years like he loves his own body.

That he will love his wife like God loves his Church.
With God all things are possible.

13. We would write down the financial plans for our future
concerning future expenses or items. We each knew that
our daily task was to operate our household. Both of us were
flexible and made sacrifices when certain things came up.
Our goal was to make a happy home and do any job that
had to be done together.

(Ephesians 5:21, 23-33, KJV)

^{23} For the **husband is the head of the wife**, even as Christ is the
head of the church: and he is the saviour of the body.

^{24} Therefore as the church is subject unto Christ, so let the wives be
to their own husbands in every thing.

^{25} **Husbands, love your wives**, even as Christ also loved the church,
and gave himself for it;

^{26} That he might sanctify and cleanse it with the washing of water
by the word,

^{27} That he might present it to himself a glorious church, not having
spot, or wrinkle, or any such thing; but that it should be holy and
without blemish.

^{28} **So ought men to love their wives as their own bodies**. He that
loveth his wife loveth himself.

^{29} For no man ever yet hated his own flesh; but nourisheth and
cherisheth it, even as the Lord the church:

^{30} For we are members of his body, of his flesh, and of his bones.

[31] For this cause shall a man leave his father and mother, and shall be joined unto his wife, and they two shall be one flesh.

[32] This is a great mystery: but I speak concerning Christ and the church.

[33] Nevertheless let every one of you in particular so love his wife even as himself; and the wife see that she reverence her husband.

(Colossians 3:19, KJV)

[19] Husbands, love your wives, and be not bitter against them.

Husbands, love your wives, and do not be harsh with them. Just because you are the Head of the House you can not be bitter, harsh, towards your wife or children. You have to love your wife until she has no doubt at all that you love her like Christ loves His Church. Husbands are likewise given spiritual obligations towards their wives. This includes demonstrating the same selfless, sacrificial love and concern shown by Christ for the church (Ephesians 5:25).

(Hebrews 13:4, KJV)

[4] Marriage is honourable in all, and the bed undefiled: but whoremongers and adulterers God will judge.

Marriage is honorable and ordained by God. The marriage bed is undefiled and pure. It is a beautiful thing to love one another in spirit and in the physical. God wants us to enjoy one another in our marriage bed. Husband is to love his wife sexually and no one else. The wife is to do the same. God will judge the sexually immoral and adulterers.

(1 Peter 3:7, KJV)

⁷ Likewise, ye husbands, dwell with them according to knowledge, giving honour unto the wife, as unto the weaker vessel, and as being heirs together of the grace of life; that your prayers be not hindered.

Husbands are to live with their wives in an understanding way, showing honor to the wife as the weaker vessel. Weaker physically since you are her protector. This is very important to God because if you do not treat your wife with love, understanding, and knowledge, God will not hear your prayers. God wants us to get along and be happily married. If you want to live a happy life and see good years, you will refrain your tongue from speaking evil to or about your wife. If you do not know how to bridle your tongue, you deceive your own heart and your religion is in vain. Salvation, charity, and love began in your home with your wife. I was accustomed to fussing all the time when I first got married. I was nineteen years old, spoiled, and wanted to have my way. My husband used wisdom as the Head of the House; and would not fuss back at me. Instead he would tell me in such a calm way that how I was acting was wrong. He would pray for me and do something nice for me. It takes two people to have a real argument. Therefore, there would be no arguments in our house. After a while I felt stupid for throwing a tantum all by myself. I was childish and my husband had great patience with me, he had to help advise me to be an obedience, calm, sweet, and sensible wife. We are a working team as husband and wife to get to Heaven together.

As mentioned before, a Man of God will love his wife as his own body. He will nourish and cherish his wife as the Lord loves and cherishes the Church. A Leader will leave his father and mother, join his wife, and they shall be one flesh.

A holy Man will dwell with his wife with knowledge; he knows that it is vital! His home and marriage should be happy and flow like the Word of God says. A leader will be committed and will surrender to the order of the Lord. He will live with his wife and take his place as the head of the house. The husband will work and provide for her and seek God for the necessary tools to help his wife grow and mature spiritually. He will protect, care, and show her that his love will cover all misunderstandings. By his actions, he will show her that he adores, loves, and cares very much for her. As a husband he will seek God how to understand his wife, which takes a lot of patience. It is very hard to understand a wife during certain times in her life. However, the leader will have much patience, compassion, kindness, and tenderness towards his wife. This saved man will seek the help of Our Savior, give his wife honor with high respect, and great esteem. A Man of God knows that his wife may be physically weaker by lacking physical strength and energy. Also, he recognizes that she is delicate and more emotional than he is, which is why he will always be her covering. He understands she is the weaker vessel and does not think or react like him. However, he realizes that she is a gift from God and very valuable to him. This Holy Man has a great responsibility in his marriage. As mentioned before, he is the one that makes sure his wife knows without a shadow of doubt that he loves her as God loves the Church. The husband will always put her first right after God. When a leader really loves his wife with all his heart, his wife will respond to that love by obeying him and loving him more.

A real Man of God and a Good Husband.

(I Timothy 3:1-13, KJV) **has the full job description of a Bishop and Deacon.** (Titus 2:1, KJV) **state that aged men be sober, grave, temperate, sound in faith, in charity, in patience.**

(Titus 2:6,7, 8,10, KJV) Young men be sober minded. In all things shewing themselves a pattern of good works; in doctrine shewing incorruptness, gravity, sincerity, sound speech, that cannot be condemned; that he that is of the contrary part may be ashamed, <u>having no evil thing to say of you</u>. Not <u>purloining</u>, but shewing all good <u>fidelity</u>; that they may adorn the doctrine of God our Savior in all things.

<u>Purloining</u>: means steal something.

<u>Fidelity:</u> means faithfulness to a person, cause, or belief, demonstrating continuing loyalty, support, reliability, trustworthiness, dependability.

THIRTEEN

(FROM THE WIFE'S PERSPECTIVE) REASONS WHY I BELIEVE I'VE BEEN HAPPILY MARRIED

I WROTE THIS TWENTY-FIVE YEARS AGO FOR A MARRIAGE SEMINAR

1. I MARRIED A VERY SAVED, KIND, LOVING, AND UNDERSTANDING MAN.
2. WE BECAME EACH OTHER'S FRIEND FIRST, THEN AND NOW WE ARE STILL BEST FRIENDS.
3. BEST FRIENDS KNOW WHEN THEIR FRIEND IS UPSET AND WITH LOVE WILL PERSIST IN FINDING OUT WHAT'S WRONG AND HOW THEY CAN HELP. *NEVER SAY TO YOUR BEST FRIEND, THERE IS NOTHING WRONG. IT IS OKAY TO SAY THERE IS SOMETHING WRONG, BUT I'M TOO UPSET TO TALK ABOUT IT RIGHT NOW, WE CAN TALK ABOUT IT LATER.
4. BEST FRIENDS TELL ONE ANOTHER EVERYTHING. WE HAVE ALWAYS COMMUNICATED WITH ONE ANOTHER AND ABLE TO TELL EACH OTHER ANYTHING. WE DISCUSS THINGS SUCH AS DEEP THOUGHTS, FEELINGS, FEARS, HIDDEN INFERIOR PROBLEMS, HURTS, JOYS, AND HORRORS OF THE PAST, PRESENT, AND FUTURE.
5. WE CAN ALWAYS TELL ONE ANOTHER THE PROS AND CONS, FAULTS, IMPERFECTIONS, AND

THINGS WE DO THAT IRRITATE EACH OTHER WITHOUT BLOWING IT OUT OF PROPORTION.

   a. THE WAY YOU TELL A SPOUSE THEIR FAULTS IS TO PICK A SPECIAL TIME AND SAY IT WITH LOVE. IT IS ALRIGHT TO CRITICIZE WITHOUT BEING HARSHLY CRITICAL. IN YOUR CRITICIZING, YOU CAN DO IT IN A LOVING WAY THAT THE OPPOSITE SPOUSE WILL SAY, I WILL WORK ON THAT AREA IN MY LIFE TO DO BETTER.

   b. TAKE TIME TO TRUTHFULLY EVALUATE ONE ANOTHER. EVEN THE BEST MARRIAGE CAN BE BETTER. SO, LEARN HOW TO DISCUSS HOW TO MAKE YOUR MARRIAGE BETTER.

6. BEST FRIENDS ACCEPT EACH OTHER AS THEY ARE. THERE MAY BE IRRITATING THINGS ABOUT ONE ANOTHER, BUT LEARN TO LIVE WITH IT IF THEY ARE UNABLE TO CHANGE AND LOVE THEM ANYWAY. ALSO, REMEMBER THERE ARE SOME THINGS IN A PERSON THAT MIGHT TAKE YEARS TO CHANGE. BE PATIENT!

7. LEARN TO GO THROUGH UNBEARABLE HARD TIMES WITHOUT BLAMING EACH OTHER FOR THE BAD TIMES. INSTEAD, LEARN HOW TO ENCOURAGE, LOVE, AND COMFORT ONE ANOTHER FOR STICKING TOGETHER THROUGH THE BAD TIMES.

8. ESTABLISH A COMMON INTEREST. OUR'S ARE:

   A. SERVING THE LORD

   B. PREACHING

   C. TEACHING

   D. ENCOURAGING GOD'S PEOPLE TO HOLD ON

   E. SNATCHING AS MANY SOULS AS WE CAN FROM THE GATES OF HELL

F. PRAYING TOGETHER

G. FASTING TOGETHER

H. STUDYING GOD'S WORD TOGETHER

I. GOING TO CHURCH TOGETHER

J. WE LOVE CRUISES, TIME SHARES, AND HOTELS

K. GOING TO ROMANTIC PLACES

L. WE LOVE FANCY RESTAURANTS

M. TRAVELING

N. WATCHING OUR FAVORITE SHOWS TOGETHER

9. ALWAYS TAKE TIME OUT FOR ONE ANOTHER, WHILE THE CHILDREN ARE AT THE BABY SITTER. WHEN WE WERE POOR, WE WENT TO THE PARK FOR PICNICS OR FAST FOOD RESTARANT'S BECAUSE WE COULD NOT AFFORD TO GO TO FANCY RESTAURANTS. WE HAVE ALWAYS SENT CARDS AND SMALL GIFTS TO EACH OTHER. THERE ISN'T AN OCCASION THAT ONE FLOWER, ONE CANDY BAR, OR A CARD HAVE NOT MADE US CLOSER. THERE ARE TIMES WHEN HE BUYS ME MANY CARDS TO EXPRESS HIS LOVE FOR ME! I ALSO DO THE SAME. WE ALWAYS THINK ABOUT AND DO FOR ONE ANOTHER ON HOLIDAYS. WHEN WE BECAME FINANCIALLY STABLE, WE BEGAN TO GO TO MORE ELABORATE RESTAURANTS, HOTELS, AND GIVE BETTER GIFTS.

10. MY HUSBAND ALWAYS HAS MY BEST INTEREST IN MIND AND I
RECIPRICATE. WE BOTH TRY TO ALWAYS THINK OF THE OTHER MORE THAN WE DO OURSELVES.

11. WE GO ABOVE AND BEYOND TO MAKE EACH OTHER HAPPY. WE CONSTANTLY MAKE ONE ANOTHER FEEL LIKE OUR MARRIAGES IS THE

MOST IMPORTANT IN OUR LIVES, WITH THE EXCEPTION OF THE LORD BEING FIRST.

12. LAUGHTER: THE BIBLE DECLARES THAT LAUGHTER IS LIKE MEDICINE. LEARN TO LAUGH! DON'T TAKE LIFE, TROUBLE, OR MISFORTUNE TO HEART. NONE OF US ARE EQUIPPED TO FIX EVERYTHING IN OUR LIVES, SO STOP BEING SO SERIOUS! JUST FORGET IT AND GO ON! TRY TO LAUGH IT OFF AND SAY IN (I -5) YEARS FROM NOW WE WOULD HAVE FORGOTTEN ALL ABOUT IT, OR WE'LL STILL BE LAUGHING ABOUT IT, SO WHY NOT LAUGH NOW! INSTEAD OF WAITING FOR YEARS FROM NOW, LAUGH NOW! LEARN TO HAVE FUN WITH ONE ANOTHER. LAUGH AND HAVE FUN NOW! LEARN TO MAKE EACH OTHER LAUGH.

13. HAVE RESPECT ONE FOR ANOTHER. LEARN TO SAY I'M SORRY EVEN IF YOU ARE IN THE RIGHT. IT IS EASY FOR A MISUNDERSTANDING TO GO TOO FAR AND YOUR MARRIAGE ENDS UP ON THE ROCKS. IT DOES NOT MATTER WHO IS RIGHT OR WRONG, BOTH OF YOU APOLOGIZE AND GO ON!

14. I PRAISE GOD BECAUSE MY HUSBAND HAS ALWAYS CARRIED HIMSELF IN A WAY THAT I CAN RESPECT HIM. HE NEVER RAISES HIS VOICE, CALL ME NAMES, PUSH, SHOVE, SLAP, OR HIT ME. HIS BEHAVIOR EXEMPLIFIED A REAL MAN OF GOD. *REAL MEN NEVER HIT OR SLANDER A WOMAN. HE IS DEMEANOR AND ACTIONS ARE LOVING. I LOVE OBEYING MY HUSBAND BECAUSE HIS CHARACTER MAKES IT EASY TO OBEY AND SUBMIT.

15. IT IS IMPORTANT TO TRUST ONE ANOTHER TOTALLY IN EVERYTHING AND EVERYWAY. THE FINANCES COMING INTO THE HOUSE IS NEVER MY MONEY OR HIS MONEY, BUT OUR MONEY!

16. IT IS ALSO IMPERITIVE TO LET THE BUSINESS-MINDED SPOUSE TAKE CARE OF THE BILLS. NEVER BUY ANYTHING EXPENSIVE WITHOUT FIRST CONSULTING AND DISCUSSING IT WITH EACH OTHER. TEACH THE SPOUSE THAT DOESN'T UNDERSTAND BUSINESS SO THAT IF THE BUSINESS-MINDED SPOUSE GOES HOME TO BE WITH THE LORD, THE ONE THAT REMAINS WILL KNOW WHERE EVERYTHING IS AND CAN CONTINUE THE TRANSACTIONS AND BILLS.

17. NEVER ALLOW THIRD PARTIES INTO YOUR MARRIAGE EXCEPT WHEN BOTH OF YOU AGREE TO CONSULT WITH A PASTOR OR CHURCH COUNSELOR THAT WON'T TAKE SIDES. DON'T TALK ABOUT YOUR SPOUSE WHEN YOU ARE ANGRY WITH HIM/HER OR TO A THIRD PARTY. WHEN YOU SAY THINGS IN ANGER, YOU DON'T REALLY MEAN IT, BECAUSE YOU MAGNIFY HIS/HER FAULTS IN ANGER. WHEN YOU MAKE-UP, YOU WILL FORGET ALL THE THINGS YOU SAID ABOUT HIM/HER. HOWEVER, YOUR FAMILY, FRIENDS, OR THIRD PARTIES WILL NOT FORGET WHAT YOU SAID. THEY WILL ALWAYS HOLD IT AGAINST YOUR MATE. IF YOU ARE GOING THROUGH BAD TIMES, KEEP IT IN YOUR MARRIAGE. DON'T COMPLAIN, BUT ENCOURAGE ONE ANOTHER. DON'T BELITTLE A MAN WHEN HE IS DOWN OR HAVE LOST HIS JOB, INSTEAD ENCOURAGE HIM! WHEN HE GETS ON HIS FEET AGAIN THERE WILL BE NOTHING

HE WILL NOT DO FOR YOU! *PLEASE DO NOT RECEIVE ANY FALSE GARBAGE ABOUT YOUR SPOUSE FROM ANYONE.

18. WE CONTINUE TO BE COURTEOUSE AND SAY THANK YOU AND PLEASE TO ONE ANOTHER. WHEN YOU SAY PLEASE AND THANK YOU, YOU'RE DISPLAYING KINDNESS AND RESPECT. THAT'S A SIGN OF PROPER MANNERS. THOSE SIMPLE TWO WORDS ARE THE MOST BASIC WORDS TO LET YOUR SPOUSE KNOW HOW IMPORTANT THEY ARE AND THAT YOU ARE NOT TAKING THEM FOR GRANTED. ALWAYS BE THANKFUL FOR WHATEVER YOU HAVE WHETHER IT IS HOT DOGS AND BEANS COMPARED TO SOMEONE'S STEAK. TELL EACH OTHER THANK YOU FOR WHAT HE/SHE HAS DONE AND FOR BEING YOU'RE SPOUSE.

19. LET ONE ANOTHER KNOW IT IS NOT THE MATERIAL THINGS THAT MAKE YOU HAPPY, BUT IT IS ONE ANOTHER! IF YOU ARE HAPPY AND APPRECIATE EACH OTHER WHEN YOU ARE POOR, WHEN GOD RICHLY BLESSES YOU, YOU WILL ALREADY KNOW HOW TO BE HAPPY!

20. WE NEVER TOOK THE ROMANCE OUT OF OUR MARRIAGE! WE WORK HARD TO KEEP THE FLAMES BURNING BRIGHT. STAY ON YOUR HONEYMOON!!!

FOURTEEN

(Husband's Perspective) Reasons Why My Husband is Happily Married.

MY HUSBAND WROTE THIS TWENTY-FIVE YEARS AGO

THE REASONS WHY I HAVE HAD A HAPPY MARRIAGE:

1. OUR MARRIAGE IS ORDAINED BY GOD
2. WE HAVE OPEN COMMUNICATION
3. I AIM TO PLEASE
4. I LOVE TO MAKE MY WIFE HAPPY.
5. WE TAKE TIME FOR EACH OTHER (VACATIONS WITH NO CHILDREN AND NO ADULTS, NO DOGS, NO CATS, JUST THE TWO OF US). THIS ALSO ENABLES US TO MAINTAIN OUR SANITY IN THE MIDST OF THE HUSTLE AND BUSTLE OF LIFE.
6. WE ARE QUITE OPPOSITE OF EACH OTHER (FOR EXAMPLE: IF THE HOUSE WAS ON FIRE, MY WIFE WOULD BE SCREAMING, JUMPING, AND QUITE HISTORICAL; I WOULD PROBABLY CALMLY SAY, "LET'S GO NEXT DOOR AND CALL THE FIREMAN, THEY WILL BE HERE SHORTLY".
7. I'M LIKE A TOWER OF STRENGTH FOR MY WIFE, SOMEBODY SHE CAN LEAN ON NATURALLY AND SPIRITUALLY.
8. I HAVE A WIFE WHO IS SUBMISSIVE AND VERY OBEDIENT TO ME.

9. I CONDUCT MYSELF IN SUCH A WAY AS HEAD OF THE HOUSEHOLD, THE HUSBAND. MY WIFE HAS NO PROBLEM SUBMITTING OR BEING OBEDIENT.
10. MY WIFE HAS HELD ON TO ME THROUGH THICK AND THIN, IN SICKNESS AND HEALTH, FOR BETTER FOR WORSE, FOR RICHER OR FOR POORER, IN SUNSHINE AND RAIN.
11. WE ENCOURAGE EACH OTHER.
12. THE UNQUENCHABLE LOVE OF GOD AND THE UNQUENCHABLE LOVE FOR EACH OTHER IS THE SOLID, UNDERLYING REASON FOR OUR HAPPY MARRIAGE.

FIFTEEN

HUSBANDS/ HAPPY 47TH ANNIVERSARY

Do your job as a Holy Man of God as written in the Bible and love your wife like your own flesh. Your wife will be able to say these things about you below, which I wrote to my husband on our Anniversary, Valentine's Day, and his Birthday.

This part of the letter I wrote to him on our Anniversary. I really wrote a book about forty-seven years of happiness.

HAPPY 47TH ANNIVERSARY (1/3/2021)

Some people go out for dinner, give gifts, and go to hotels on their anniversary. They do these things because society says this is the day to do this for your wife or husband on your anniversary. This day and every day you have proven to me that God ordained our union and marriage. Forty-seven years is a very long time to stay with the same person under the same roof. Forty-seven years I have been your wife and you have been my husband. Forty-seven years have really gone by fast because we have always had fun together no matter what would happen to us. We always counted on Jesus and our love for each other. We have been an unbreakable Team. I could always count on you as being my true lifelong friend. Forty-seven years I have been able to tell you my dreams, thoughts, and concerns and you would always listen. Forty-seven years is a long time for a man to remain the same. You have not changed towards me. We have laughed a lot about growing old together. Things always went better when I was with you. I am happier when we are together.

I would like to let you know how much I still appreciate you taking me to see my sister. You have the most wonderful, kind, gentle, and considerate spirit. I will always have a deeper love and appreciation for you because you took me to see my sister before she died. You did not say "We do not have the money" or "Let me think about it" you said "YES". Most men are not caring, kind, gentle, and considerate like you. It is so easy to live with you.

I would like to thank you again for being a "Strong Tower" for me when we had to move and after we moved. You have a great understanding of me. You are so compassionate towards me. I think living with me has given you a great wisdom of women. I love how you understand me and have always known how to talk to me. You are a "GIANT" of a man. You are the "STRONGEST" man I have ever met. You are "AWESOME". Words cannot express the wholeness of you. You are always the same at home. The same sweet, kind, gentle, considerate, and wonderful man I married forty-seven years ago. The only change I see in you is that you have done and said more powerful things of God.

You love to sit close to me. That makes me feel wanted, special, and safe. You find me soon as you come home and you hug me. Actually, you hug me almost every time you pass me in the house. You hug me more now than ever in our marriage life. All of these things are not changing but just added on to the affection from the beginning of our marriage.

I know it has not been easy but you have given me more than any man could give his wife. I have your undivided attention on!!!FRIDAYS!!! !!!SWEET FRIDAYS!!! A special day devoted for me. Thank you so much. Our "FRIDAYS" have helped me more than you will ever know. FRIDAYS!!! SWEET FRIDAYS!!! has given me more than any doctor or pill could do for me. You have accomplished something I have longed for all my marriage life. Thank you once again. I know you are the busiest man in Tidewater, but thank you for making time for me and "US". Thank you so much for taking me to the ZOO and every time we stayed in a Bed and Breakfast on eastern shore. They were heavenly trips with you on the ocean. I will never forget our boat ride to Tangier Island and sitting on the picnic bench in your arms looking at the ocean. You have given me Life Time Memories that will sooth my mind, heart, and soul when I think of them.

You have proven your love for me for **forty-seven** years. I want to thank you for being so special to me and loving me through all **forty-seven** years. I thank God because you are sweet, kind, considerate, and loving towards my daughter and me. You and I being together makes me happy. Regardless of where we are or whom we are with, I feel happy with you. Your love for me and the love I have and share with you can stand up against anyone in this world. As long as I have your love, the hate that people throw my way does not matter. Our love is greater than anything in this world. Our love is better than a soap opera, love story in a book, or in a movie. All of those love scenes are from a script and they are getting paid to act. What we have is so deep and real because God ordained our love and our marriage. Again, it is easy so easy to love you. It is so easy to live with you and obey you.

- THANK YOU for being a saved, sanctified man before me in my home.
- Thank you for always working and taking care of me.
- Thank you for always working and taking care of Shekinah when she lived with us.
- Thank you for always paying the mortgage, water, electricity, and every other bill on time.
- Thank you for never allowing me to worry about not even "ONE" bill in **forty-seven** years.
- Thank you for being the best covering a wife could have.

- Thank you for being the master of your home and church.
- Thank you for being the strongest man on the planet.
- Thank you for being absolutely faithful to me as your wife.
- Thank you for showing me your power and strength to instruct your household in righteousness and holiness.
- Thank you for still loving me and being thoughtful and kind when I am going through the Big "M". The Big "M" is (MENOPAUSE).
- Thank you for putting bottled water on my nightstand for me.
- Thank you for bringing me bananas without me asking for them. It makes me know you are still thinking about me when you are away from me.
- Thank you for tucking me into bed for **forty-seven** years.
- Thank you for making sure Shekinah had the best health insurance when she lived with us.
- Thank you for making sure I had the best health insurance. Thank you for still loving me and being kind to me even when my health insurance was very expensive. You have never treated me bad for all the doctor bills, doctor visits, medicines, and sicknesses I had which was many.
- Thank you for letting my mom stay with us until she died. You always treated my mom wonderful and never complained, not even once for her staying with us for fifteen years.
- Thank you for showing me how much God loves me through the love and care you show Shekinah and I every day of our life.
- Thank you for loving me as you love your own body.
- Thank you for nourishing and cherishing me until I became a woman as I stand now strong.
- Thank you for dwelling with me according to knowledge, love, understanding, and compassion and giving honor to me as the weaker vessel.

- Thank you for always making me laugh, I have so much fun with you.
- Thank you for the love you have for me which has grown stronger, deeper, and more intensely than you did **forty-seven** years ago.
- Thank you for making my daughter and me feel loved every day of our life.
- Thank you for being you, I could not ask God for a better husband, companion, or friend. You are the Greatest in this whole wide world.
- All good things come from God. Truly, I have received you from the Lord.
- Thank you for being "STRONG" through the storms, hurricanes, tornadoes, and uncertain times. You keep on going like the energizer bunny.
- Thank you for telling me that it is not my fault that I am sickly, that you are not like other
- people, that I can tell you anytime how I feel in my body. You are Priceless.
- Now that I am older, and have more sick days, thank you for telling me that you are my Care-Taker, you love me, and love caring for me. You are Precious.
- Thank you for laughing about some of these changes in Life as we age.
- Thank you for growing old with me and taking all the side effects of old age together.
- Thank you for telling me we just have to help each other.
- Thank you for loving and treating me so wonderful, that we have become one together. This is an extremely happy married life, which God intended.
- I LOVE YOU JOHN SIMENSKY HARRELL

Love Your Loving Wife

SIXTEEN

I HAVE GOTTEN A MAN
FROM THE LORD!!!!!

A Letter I wrote to my husband. (2/14/2021)

Some people are giving valentine candy and cards today because society says this is the day to do this for your sweet heart. This day and every day you are my Valentine and I know I am yours.

You have proven your love for me for forty-seven years. I want to thank you for being so special to me and loving me through all forty-seven years. I cry sometimes because how sweet, kind, gentle, considerate, and loving you are to my daughter and me. I have Jesus and you, that is enough to continue to make me overjoyed with joy and love until Jesus returns. I do not need anything but you. You are the only one I want and need. You and I together make me happy. Regardless of where we are, or whom we are with, I feel complete with you. Your love for me and the love I have and share with you, it can stand up against anyone in this world. As long as I have your love, the hate that people throw my way it does not matter. Our love is greater than anything in this world. Our love is better than a soap opera, love story in a book, or in a movie because all of the love scenes are from a script and they are paid to do it. What we have is so deep and real because God ordained our love and our marriage. Again, it is so easy to love you. It is so easy to live and obey you. Your very presence in my life makes me whole, happy, and complete. I love you so much, I sit down at times thinking what must I do to let him feel and see the love I have for him. I am drop down, mad silly in love with you! You make it so that I do not need to look for a cure.

I love loving you and I love how we love each other. You are more than just a husband, Pastor, Bishop, lover, and companion, you are the very best friend I have in this world. The only other person I love more is Jesus. I would do anything in this world for you. I would give you everything you desire and much, much, much, much, much, much, much, much, much, much, much, much, much, much, more.

Words cannot express how I love and appreciate you. I hope my everyday actions show you how much I love you. I love you a zillion times more than when I said "I DO" to you **forty-seven** years ago.

- THANK YOU for being a saved sanctified man before me in my home.
- Thank you for always working and taking care of me.
- Thank you for always working and taking care of Shekinah when she lived with us.
- Thank you for always paying the mortgage, water, electricity and every other bill on time.
- Thank you for never allowing me to worry about "ONE" bill in **forty-seven** years.
- Thank you for being the best covering a wife could have.
- Thank you for being the master of your home and church.
- Thank you for being the strongest man on the planet.
- Thank you for being absolute faithful to me as your wife.
- Thank you for showing me your power and strength to instruct your household in righteousness and holiness.
- Thank you for demonstrations how much God loves me through the love and care you show Shekinah and I every day of our life.
- Thank you for loving me as you love your own body.
- Thank you for nourishing and cherishing me until I became a stronger woman.

- Thank you for dwelling with me according to knowledge, love, understanding, compassion, and giving honor to me as the weaker vessel.
- Thank you for always making me laugh and I have so much fun with you!
- I feel your love for me even stronger, deeper, and more intensely than you did forty-seven years ago, thank you.
- Thank you for being you! I could not ask God for a better husband, lover, companion, or friend! You are the Greatest in this whole wide world!
- Thank you for loving and treating me so wonderful! That we have become one. This is an extremely happy married life, which God intended.
- Thank you for going to the doctors with me, holding my hand, praying for me and quoting scripture until I became calm.

I LOVE YOU JOHN SIMENSKY HARRELL

SEVENTEEN

A LETTER TO MY HUSBAND
FOR HIS BIRTHDAY

HAPPY BIRTHDAY

2/26/2021

Today, after leaving the doctors I thought I would go and get you a Father's Day card. However, I decided to get a letter that I had written to you June 2006. Nothing has changed except you are even more awesome! You are Special! You are the Best! You are #1. You are the best Father and Husband in the whole world. As I went through the selection of cards, I kept picking up cards that expressed exactly how I felt about you. The young lady that was at the cashier actually came in the aisle and looked at me because I was reading cards and making sounds of approval about the cards. As I was checking out, she asked me what kind of a man deserve five Father's Day cards.

I told her that my husband was the most wonderful, kind, exceptional man I have ever met in my entire life. He is a wonderful husband and father. I told her that I had been happily married to you for thirty-two years, my daughter had completed three years of college and for her 21st birthday he took the whole family and a friend on a week Caribbean cruise. Then as I left, I said he is really saved and I would do anything for him. There is nothing I would not do for him. I emphasized; I MEAN NOTHING, I WOULD NOT DO FOR HIM.

As I sit in my car for a few minutes, I realized the cards expressed how I felt; yet what I said to the cashier was true. However, the real reason I love and adore you is because you know my daughter and me. You have taken the time to know and understand me better than I understand myself. You married a nineteen-year-old that was spoiled and had to grow up. And you were man enough and spiritual enough to help me mature mentally, spiritually, and become a complete and whole woman of God.

You were poor financially when I first married you, yet you were so rich in God, wisdom, and love. I know you came from God. I would drive around and cry like a baby because God gave you to me. I have loved you from the first time we ate together at the Chinese Restaurant. I did not know what was wrong with me, yet everyone else knew. You made me laugh, smile, and feel so good inside like no other human being. One encounter with you touched and changed me. You brought the best out of me when I was with you, or through your letters, and telephone calls. You inspired me to be better, happier, and to be the best I could possibly be on this earth. Your unconditional love for my daughter and me has been heavenly right here on earth. The love you have allowed us to see, feel, and share between us has protected us. It covered us both from the evils, hates, dislikes, disapprovals, and the emps that the devil has sent our way. Your precious love has been enough. It is not a joke when I say I got Jesus and John and that is enough. I do not say it because it sounds cute, I say it because it is true! All I need is Jesus and you!

Today, as I drove to the YMCA with my daughter, she told me that she did not take our family for granted. She said that she thanked God how we love each other, how we laugh and have fun together. She told me that she realized many other families do not have a close relationship. She noticed a lot of families have drama in their family life. These words were priceless coming from a 21-year-old girl.

You have been the glue that has kept us together as a loving family. It has taken more work on your part to bring our family this far. You have poured so much of yourself in us that I am proud to say my daughter has most of your ways. My emotions have calmed down and have learned to deal with life more like you. You have always loved us; you've had always been there when we needed you and you have always made our life as a family so special. We love just being with you. You are much more than just a man, husband, and father. You are a husband, father, a very best friend, an unpaid counselor for Shekinah and me, a healer of a broken heart, counselor, Pastor, Bishop, doctor, and watchman for our life and soul. You are the source of our strength next to God.

It is not the diamonds, furs, or things you have given me. I have deeply loved you when you could only afford to give me snicker bars. My mother prayed that I would get a good husband. I could not have prayed or chosen a better husband than you. You are a part of me. I was born and made for you and you were born and made for me. There is not a book or movie that can even come close to the love and devotion that we share as husband, wife, and daughter. We have shared many trails and tribulations, yet it has all made us closer, deeper, and more appreciative of our love for one another.

Shekinah and I are glad to be sharing our life with you. The times that we spend together as husband and wife or time together as a family is priceless! It makes everything else that this world dishes out to us insignificant. I know without a doubt, that you, our love, marriage, and family are the most important parts of my life. I told you I do not want to imagine how it would be without you. I want to die first. The thought of living without you is unbearable, that is why I want you to never doubt how I feel about you and know how much happier I am because you are in my life.

LOVE YOUR DEVOTED WIFE JUDY

EIGHTEEN

A Letter to My Husband on Father's Day

HAPPY FATHER'S DAY (2016)

TO MY WONDERFUL HUSBAND

You have been the perfect husband and father for forty-two years. My daughter and I know you love us. You have proved it for thirty-one years for my daughter and forty-two years to me. I cannot imagine living without you. You have always paid the bills for forty-two years. I never had to worry about my rent, water, vepco, gas, or any bill being paid. So many women cannot say that. I have lived a worry-free life when it comes to you taking care of our family. I never stressed over a car. When you thought I needed a new car, it would be parked in front of our house. You have always taken excellent care of me and our daughter. You always allowed us dress nicely. Food and clothing were never a concern. You have always taken good care of us. You kept gas in my car, registration updated, repaired, and inspections up to part. You have spoiled me for years. I don't even think about looking at the gas gauge because you always maintained it. When it comes to living, you have made it very easy for my daughter and me. You never wanted me to worry about anything in life. Having such an excellent covering for the both of us touches my heart. You would go to Shekinah's job and make sure her car has the things that it needs. You have an incredible mind that keeps up with everything that involves us and the church. I thank the Lord for you because you came from God. Every good and perfect gift comes from above. I love how you constantly remain calm, even while taking care of disasters and problems. Thank you for knowing how to calm me down when I was nervous about situations! You could make me laugh when I had been crying. In the worst of times, you have always been a strong tower for the both of us. The way you love me and my daughter is better than any book or movie because they are acting, but you are for real. I feel at times you get tired of me telling you that you are so sweet and the greatest husband in the world. That is a testimony in itself. I have been married to you for forty-two years and I am still in awe about you. I live with you, but it is an incredible experience to observe you deal with life. I enjoy how we love each other and spend time with each other. I love how we talk, laugh, and have fun with each other. God has truly given us a great, priceless gift! God joined us to love and cherish one another. Every day I am amazed about you. You have shown me great love and compassion for years. I appreciate the way you took care of me when I was sick. You have never been mean to me or acted like you were tired of me. When you had to wash me and put on my clothes, that was the day I knew I would take a bullet for you. I can never express how wonderful you are. I try to show you how much I love and appreciate you by gladly obeying you and doing whatever you ask of me. I am most happy when I am doing something for you. You take time out for me or accompany me to take difficult, painful, long medical tests. It always goes better with you! I am eternally grateful for you sitting next to me, praying, quoting scriptures, and holding my hand to get through hours of tests. There is not a husband in the world like you. Our love for one another is impeccable. I feel the deep love you have for me every time you fill my water bottles, bring me food, tuck me into bed, opening my car door, and do special things to make sure I 'm comfortable. You make me feel special! This is no act; you have been doing things like this for me our entire marriage. We are blessed and we do not take each other for granted. Like the waitress said at Shoney's, we act like newlyweds! Yes, that is how we have acted for forty-two years. That is a great gift God has given us. We are truly blessed with happiness with each other. We have loved our daughter and she is just a great expression of our love together. It makes my heart feel glad every time our daughter tells me that she feels loved at all times. She is such a happy young lady because she came up in a home that was filled with love. I thank God with all my heart that the three of us are so joyous and love each other. This is another jewel God has given us. We love and support each other all the time. Thank you, Jesus, again, for the greatest husband and father on Earth. All good things come from God; my husband, my daughter, our love, and our fellowship, came from God. If I was rich, I would give you so much to you. For now, I give you my love, my affection, and myself to you. I wish you a Happy Father's Day to the greatest, awesome, wonderful, amazing, astonishing, magnificent husband and father on the entire planet Earth.

I want to thank you from the bottom of my heart how you always were good to my family. You did wonderful things that most men would not have done. I want to tell you I love you a trillion times more for how you drove me to the hospital and stayed with me to take care of a family member. My heart will always love you for that. You are a one of a kind man. When God made you, He broke the mold. However, we are praying that God will create a husband for Shekinah like you!

Love,
Your faithful wife,
Judy

P. S. As I sit and typed this letter about you, my heart just exploded with love until I shed tears as my heart typed about you. I Love you so much!!!

LAST CHAPTER

ONLY FOR WOMEN THAT MARRY HOLY MEN AND ARE VERY SERIOUS ABOUT PLEASING GOD.

Only a few women in the 21th Century can handle these words that are in the Bible. I went to a church and God lead me to teach this. You did not have to have discernment to see how most of the women did not receive this word and were very upset.

Wife Submit to Your Husband:

<u>SUBMIT:</u> MEANS TO ACCEPT OR YIELD TO A SUPERIOR FORCE (YOUR HUSBAND) OR

ACCEPT THE AUTHORITY OR WILL OF ANOTHER PERSON (YOUR HUSBAND)

<u>(Genesis 3:16, KJV)</u>

Unto the woman he said, I will greatly multiply thy sorrow and thy conception; in sorrow thou shalt bring forth children; and **thy desire shall be to thy husband**, and **he shall rule over thee**.

In the Garden of Eden Adam and Eve hid themselves from God because they were naked.

(Genesis 3:11, KJV) And he said, Who told thee that thou wast naked? Hast thou eaten of the tree, whereof I commanded thee that thou shouldest not eat?

Adam blamed the Woman; Eve blamed the serpent. The Lord God punish all of them. Therefore, if you are a woman of God, it should not be a problem to submit yourself to your husband **(A Man of God).** Also, your desire is going to be to please your husband, always. If you are truly saved and want to please the Lord, you will let Him manifest the desire to please your husband that He put in women since the Garden of Eden. Example: I love dressing in clothes, hats, etc. that my husband likes to see me in. I love fixing his favorite foods and decorating the house with things he really enjoys. My desire is to make him so happy at home that he is excited to come home to his palace. I know I was doing excellent job when my husband came home from work and said "I could not hardly wait to get home to you".

(Deuteronomy 24:5, KJV)

"When a man is newly married, he shall not go out with the army or be liable for any other public duty. He shall be free at home one year to be **happy with his wife** whom he has taken.

God honors marriage, He wanted a newly married man to stay home with his wife one year to enjoy his wife. God knows it takes about a year to really know one another and get all the kinks out your marriage. It takes time to learn one another's ways, likes, and dislikes. God wants all married couples to be **HAPPY** with one another. See reference in **(Proverbs 31:10-31, KJV).**

(Proverbs 12:4, KJV)

[4] A virtuous woman is a crown to her husband: but she that maketh ashamed is as rottenness in his bones.

You must be a virtuous woman as stated in **(Proverbs 31 and Proverbs 12:4, KJV)**. When you are a virtuous woman, you are a crown to your husband, you deserve the holy title of an ideal holy wife. You make your marriage blessed because of how you act in following the Word of God toward your husband. You are a good helpmate. You make him feel like a King that wears a Crown. You are the Crown.

(Proverbs 3:1 & 2, KJV)

1 My son, forget not my law; but **let thine heart keep my commandments:**

2 For **length of days**, and **long life**, and **peace**, shall they add to thee.

When your heart keeps the commandments of God and you love your husband like the Bible says **you will add length of days**, **long life, peace, Love, cheerfulness, joyfulness** will be **added to your life and marriage.**

(Ecclesiasticus 26:1, KJV)

"Blessed is the man that hath a **virtuous wife**, for the **number of his days shall be double**."

Blessed is the man that hath a good wife, for the number of his days shall be doubled. A virtuous wife will cause her husband to be joyful and he shall fulfill the years of his life in peace. A wife is a good gift. God gives a good wife to a man that fear the Lord. God did not make a woman from man's head, that she should not rule over him; nor from his feet, that she should not be his slave; but from his side, that she should be near to his heart.

(Proverbs 12:4, KJV)

[4] A virtuous woman is a crown to her husband: but **she that maketh ashamed is as rottenness in his bones.**

When you shame your husband by allowing the devil to use you by being bitter, wicked, foolish, and act like a madwoman you are rotten to his bone.

(Proverbs 18:22, KJV)

Whoso findeth a wife findeth a good thing, and obtaineth favour of the Lord.

If you are sweetly saved and filled with the Holy Ghost, you will wait until God sends you your Boaz. He will find you and love you like he loves himself. My husband found me at a Church Convention held in Baltimore, Maryland and when he was introduced to me, it was love at first sight. He lived in North Carolina and I was in Baltimore, Maryland. We wrote letters and called each other for five months and he said lets fast and pray to see if God has chosen you to be my wife. We fasted and prayed and he went to a library and held my picture up and he knew I was to be his wife before the foundation of the World. He told me since the Lord ordained us to be man and wife, let's get married. He told me he had a good reputation and he will not be sitting in my house and he did not believe in long engagements. We married in five months. We are still happily married after forty-seven years.

(Proverbs 19:14, KJV)

House and riches are the inheritance of fathers: and a **prudent** wife is from the Lord.

Prudent means a wife acting with or showing care and thought for the future of her family. Wise and well judged.

(Proverbs 21:9, KJV)

"*It is* better to dwell in a corner of the housetop, than with a brawling woman in a wide house."

Brawling means fight or quarrel in a rough or noisy way.

Let your beauty come from **your heart with a humble**, **gentle**, **kind**, and **quiet spirit**. Let your adorning be the beauty of a **gentle and quiet spirit**, which **in God's sight is very precious**.

(1 Peter 3:3-4, KJV)

³ Whose adorning let it not be that outward adorning of plaiting the hair, and of wearing of gold, or of putting on of apparel;

⁴ But let it be the hidden man of the heart, in that which is not corruptible, even the **ornament of a meek and quiet spirit, which is in the sight of God of great price.**

(1 Peter 3:5, KJV)

"For after this manner in the old time the **holy women** also, who trusted in God, **adorned themselves, being in subjection unto their own husbands:**"

In Biblical days, holy women adorned themselves in subjection unto their own husbands. It is a beautiful sight to see a holy woman love and be submissive to her husband. People call me beautiful because of my humble spirit and how I respect and obey my husband.

(Matthew 19:4-6, KJV)

[4] And he answered and said unto them, Have ye not read, that he which made them at the beginning made them male and female,

[5] And said, For this cause shall a man leave father and mother, and shall cleave to his wife: and they twain shall be one flesh?

[6] Wherefore they are no more twain, but one flesh. What therefore God hath joined together, let not man put asunder.

A man must leave his father and his mother, hold-fast to his wife like glue, and the two shall become one flesh. It takes time and patience to learn to be one flesh physically, mentally, and emotionally. The Word says you shall become **ONE FLESH**. The Word says whom God has joined together in marriage let no man or woman separate you.

When the Lord unites you with a REAL HOLY MAN and you really LOVE your husband, it is easy for charity to work in your marriage. The difficulty decreases to suffer with him in the ministry, hard times, low finance times, troublesome times.

(1 Corinthians 11:3, KJV)

[3] But I would have you know, that the head of every man is Christ; and the head of the woman is the man; and the head of Christ is God.

But I want you to understand that the head of every man is Christ, the head of a wife is her husband, and the head of Christ is God.

(1 Corinthians 6:18-20, KJV)

[18] Flee fornication. Every sin that a man doeth is without the body; but he that committeth fornication sinneth against his own body.

[19] What? know ye not that your body is the temple of the Holy Ghost which is in you, which ye have of God, and ye are not your own?

[20] For ye are bought with a price: therefore glorify God in your body, and in your spirit, which are God's.

Women of God that are saved, filled with the Holy Ghost, and married to a Man of God is to Flee from sexual immorality. Every other sin a person commits is outside the body, but the sexually immoral person sins against his own body. Your heart and body belong to your husband. Never, never ever tell another man or woman that you are having sexual problems with your husband. Speak only to your pastor's wife or a licensed Christian Counselor. Other men can sense when you are not being fulfilled. Especially an unsaved man. Keep yourself from other men at this time. Keep busy with church committees, hobbies, etc. Discuss this with your husband and ask God to keep you until you and your husband solve this problem. Sex is just as important as being submissive to your husband.

There are women in the world and also in the church waiting to hear you are having problems with your husband. Women will talk to you about how awful your husband is to you. You are unwise, if you do this. If you leave your husband, that same woman might become the next wife of your husband!

(1 Corinthians 7:1-5, 10, KJV)

7 Now concerning the things whereof ye wrote unto me: It is good for a man not to touch a woman.

[2] Nevertheless, to avoid fornication, let every man have his own wife, and let every woman have her own husband.

³ Let the husband render unto the wife due benevolence: and likewise also the wife unto the husband.

⁴ The wife hath not power of her own body, but the husband: and likewise also the husband hath not power of his own body, but the wife.

⁵ Defraud ye not one the other, except it be with consent for a time, that ye may give yourselves to fasting and prayer; and come together again, that Satan tempt you not for your incontinency.

⁶ But I speak this by permission, and not of commandment.

¹⁰ And unto the married I command, yet not I, but the Lord, Let not the wife depart from her husband:

When you are saved, it is not wise for a man to touch a woman. The flesh is weaker than you think, do not tempt the flesh. To avoid fornication, let every man have his own wife, and let every woman have her own husband. Let the husband render (give, provide, furnish, and make available) the wife due benevolence such as love, kindness, gentleness, goodness, and yes **SEX**. No husband or wife should stop having sex unless they are fasting and praying before God and both of them have agreed to that fast. The fast should only be for a short time so you can fulfill one another's sexual needs. Do not break up your own marriage because you fast and pray all the time. This kind of behavior will cause a good husband to turn to other woman for the sex that his wife would not give him. Also, this kind of behavior will cause a good wife to turn to other men for the sex that her husband would not give her. Whether you like sex or not, you can not constantly deny sex with your husband or wife. Talk to each other about this and solve this problem. If you can not solve it between each other, try going to talk to an OB/GYN, PCP, a Christian Sex Counselor, and pray for God to solve this problem.

Find out if this is a physical problem or something else. You must find out the problem and solve it.

My husband still teaches Young Pastors to make sure they do not get so busy with God's work that they forget they have a wife. She has needs just like a man. Young pastors often get so zealous with God and His work, they sin unknowingly because they neglect time with their wife. No woman is to be feeling like a single woman with a husband lying right beside her in bed. Young Pastors can be so engaged in ministry that they spend all their spare time at church, neglecting their wife and family. This is not right, Our Savior is expecting you to put Him first, but not to neglect your duties to his wife. Young Pastors have to be taught how to do this. Many young pastors lose their wives the first year of ministry because of this. It is not God's will to break up marriages. Marriage is honorable and the bed is not defiled. Ladies, please let your husband read this if he is doing this. A pastor can be overworked. This happens mainly when a pastor has a small, poor church. However, it can happen to any Pastor over a small or large congregation, no pastor can do it all. You just do your best and let God do the rest. Do not punish your wife by ignoring her, avoiding time with her, and refraining from sex. The husband should give to his wife her conjugal rights, and likewise the wife to her husband. For the wife does not have authority over her own body, but the husband does. Likewise, the husband does not have authority over his own body, but the wife does. Do not deprive one another, except perhaps by agreement for a limited time, that you may devote yourselves to fasting; but then come together again, so that Satan may not tempt you because of your lack of self-control.

Our Savior wants you to put Him first and let your wife be next. Your bodies belong to each other, and you can not be so exhausted from church work until you are too tired to date, have quality time, and be romantic with your wife. Sex is her conjugal right. This is grounds by law to get a divorce. So Young Pastors please take this seriously.

As I mentioned earlier in this book, Pastors should not talk to beautiful, attractive, good-looking, gorgeous, or plain looking woman in your study alone. Pastors have been lied on about attempting to seduce women. Therefore, keep your office door open or let your wife sit in your conference. Always keep a desk between you and a female member during conferences. You as a male Pastor should never talk to a female member about her lack of sex life with her husband. Turn her over to your wife or an elderly, consecrated mother of the church that can keep secrets.

(Ephesians 4:30, KJV)

And grieve not the holy Spirit of God, whereby ye are sealed unto the day of redemption.

Do not grieve the Holy Spirit of God by letting corrupt communication proceed out of your mouth. Do not fuss, yell, or argue with your husband. Please do not nag your husband to death. Men will work three jobs just to get away from you, so study to be quiet. When you have a disagreement, sit down like two adults, and discuss it. My husband and I look at our marriage as a Company. He is the CEO and I am the Asst. CEO. In a company when there is a conflict, you do not scream, yell, shout, or find fault in one another about it. You should sit down calmly like two mature adults and find out what the problem is and find out how to solve it. You do what is BEST for the Business; the Business is **BEING HAPPILY MARRIAGE LIKE THE BIBLE SAYS.**

(Ephesians 5:3, KJV)

[1]Be ye therefore followers of God, as dear children;

²And walk in love, as Christ also hath loved us, and hath given himself for us an offering and a sacrifice to God for a sweetsmelling savour.

³But fornication, and all uncleanness, or covetousness, let it not be once named among you, as becometh saints;

⁴Neither filthiness, nor foolish talking, nor jesting, which are not convenient: but rather giving of thanks.

⁵For this ye know, that no whoremonger, nor unclean person, nor covetous man, who is an idolater, hath any inheritance in the kingdom of Christ and of God.

⁶Let no man deceive you with vain words: for because of these things cometh the wrath of God upon the children of disobedience.

Women of God if you are a follower of God as dear children. I know you will walk in love with your husband. You will not be caught up in any of the sins listed in (**Ephesians 5:3-5, KJV**). We are loving our husbands, children, and all people because God is a God of love. We are planning to go back with the Lord in his kingdom.

<u>WIVES: I want to repeat the meaning of submit.</u>

<u>SUBMIT</u>: MEANS TO ACCEPT OR YIELD TO A SUPERIOR FORCE (YOUR HUSBAND) OR

ACCEPT THE AUTHORITY OR WILL OF ANOTHER PERSON (YOUR HUSBAND

(<u>Ephesians 5:22, KJV</u>)

<u>Wives, submit yourselves unto your own husbands</u>, as unto the Lord.

(Ephesians 5:23, KJV)

For the **husband is the head of the wife**, even as Christ is the head of the church: and he is the savior of the body.

Your husband is the head of you, the wife, even as Christ is the head of the church. When a husband has the characteristics of Christ, he is worthy of obedience and submission. He is your head, covering, protector, bodyguard, and your guardian. He is there to cover you, protect you, and conceal you from any problems or danger.

(Ephesians 5:24, KJV)

Therefore as the church is subject unto Christ, so let the wives be to their own husbands in everything.

I was young, spoiled, and I wanted things to go my way. When I was growing up, I knew some women that could, beat their husbands like a Professional Boxer. They yelled and physically fought them. My husband was a North Carolinian man, had muscles and was very strong from farm work. I knew I could not physically beat him. I did all my fighting with my tongue. I would throw tantrums when my husband said No and he meant it.

My wonderful husband had so much patience with me when I was nineteen. He knew how to talk to me and calm me down. He would never raise his voice at me when I was having a tantrum. A tantrum is an uncontrolled outburst of anger and frustration, typically in a young child. I was no longer a young child I was married and I had to mature in learning how to be subject unto my husband. He told me that he needed me to be strong in the Lord. He encouraged me to read the Bible when he went to school and work. When he came home, we walked to the church, we prayed, and he helped me tarry. Tarry means to call Jesus until He changes something in your life.

When you speak in tongues, the Holy Ghost will tell the Lord what you need. I desperately needed to grow up and be submissive to my husband. I had the Holy Ghost but I was not fervent in the Spirit. One day I threw an enormous tantrum. Instead of yelling at me, my husband went outside, washed and waxed my car, cleaned the inside, and polished my tires. That is something he never does! He always paid other people to do this for him. This was the day I began to change. I looked out the front door and watched him clean my car. This is what I told God, I said, "Lord, I have a real good husband and I am not treating him right, please help me be like him and stop fussing and throwing tantrums". I prayed and fasted often until I trained myself not to yell and get angry. This did not come over night. When I felt myself about to throw a tantrum, I would run to the bathroom and pray. I would ask the Lord to help me stop acting like a child and be mature. I prayed so hard that God began to help me. I did not have to run to the bathroom to calm down anymore. I'm a witness for any woman that is spoiled and wants her way all the time, you can change! It was in my DNA to throw tantrums, that is all I saw, inherited, and knew. However, this holy man made me ashamed of myself by doing good. I overcame the tantrums and I am so glad. It made our life so much better. Instead of throwing tantrums, I learned to discuss concerns in a nice, calm voice to explain how I felt. One day, my husband said, "Your ideas are good; however, your approached is so awful, you make a person not want to accept your ideas." I learned when my ideas were different from his, I would say "This is my idea about something, but you are the head, pray about it and whatever God leads you to do I will submit to that.

(Ephesians 5:33, KJV)

33 Nevertheless let every one of you in particular **so love his wife** even **as himself;** and the wife see that **she reverence** her **husband.**

The wife should reverence her husband.

Reverence means: **DEEP RESPECT FOR SOMEONE (YOUR HUSBAND).**

<u>**(Colossians 3:18, KJV)**</u>

<u>**Wives, submit yourselves unto your own husbands**</u>, as it is fit in the Lord.

Wives: submit, accept, and yield to your husband. Submit means to give in, give way, back down, and accept the will of your husband. Submitting also means having a voluntary attitude of cooperating, assuming responsibility, and obedience. Wives are not robots or inferior to their husbands, they are created to be cooperative helpers.

When you have a husband that loves you as he loves himself, have the characteristic of Christ, and is gentle with you, it is easy to submit yourself to him. Experiencing a caring relationship, harmony with your husband, and a home of Love makes it easy. You will be willing to let him lead the family. Your commitment and obedience towards your husband are considered "fitting" to God. The Lord is well pleased when you have a home that is operated by His standards.

<u>**(Titus 2:4,5, KJV)**</u>

(4) That they may teach the young women to be sober, to **love their husbands**, to love their children,

(5) To be discreet, chaste, keepers at home, good, <u>obedient to their own husbands, that the word of God be not blasphemed.</u>

Wives must love their husbands and children. Wives are to have self-control, be pure, working at home if possible, kind, and submissive to their own husbands. We do not want the word of God be blasphemed. Blaspheme is speaking irreverently about God or sacred things. Blaspheme also means to swear or curse against God. In order to be a good wife, it is vital not to blaspheme against Our Lord.

(1 Peter 2:13, KJV)

Submit yourselves to every ordinance of man for the Lord's sake: whether it be to the king, as supreme;

God wants you to submit yourselves to every ordinance of man. Ordinance means a piece of legislation enacted by a municipal authority. The ordinance is from the Holy Word, a Book inspired by God. Our Savior is the authority we received our commandments from. We are to submit to our kings in your homes our husbands. Marriage is an institution; the manual and instructions are in the Bible. Fast, pray, and continue to read these scriptures and you will be a submissive wife. We as woman of God are to submit and obey our husbands because we love Christ and we want to obey His Word. Therefore, it is easy to love, submit, and obey our husbands.

(1 Peter 3:1-2, KJV)

Likewise, ye wives, be in subjection to your own husbands; that, if any obey not the word, they also may without the word be won by the conversation of the wives.

(2) While they behold your chaste conversation coupled with fear.

Again, the Bible is declaring that you be in subjection to your own husband. It doesn't take much effort when he is saved, filled with the Holy Ghost, and is a great Man of God. However, this scripture is talking to woman that have unsaved husbands. If they are not saved, you still have to be holy, respect, and obey them as long as they tell you what is right. If they ask you to do ungodly things, you can not obey that. However, the King of Kings wants you be subject to your own husbands, that they may be won by your conversation, conduct, quiet spirit, love, and submission. I tell women that are married to unsaved men requires you to fast and pray more than I do. I treat my husband like a King and I do everything possible to make his life better, pleasant, and happy. I spoil him and he spoils me. I serve and cater to him like a King. In return, he treats me like a Queen. We try to outdo each other with being kind and good to one another. I've counseled women that are married to unsaved men. They have to treat their husbands with more love and kindness. Many husbands will come to the Lord from the life you live in front of them. When an unsaved man trusts his wife totally and knows she is faithful, he will brag about how sweetly saved you are and how good you are to him. I have witnessed that myself on a government job. When the unsaved husband notices how respectful you are, the way you live, and exude God's Love, he'll want to change.

During the time I worked, unsaved men would talk about how awful their wives were. Don't clean, cook, do laundry, and they just stay on the phone all day. Many of these men complained that they would leave their lazy wives if it was not for their children. Do not be in this category.

SUBJECTION: MEANS THE ACTION OF SUBJECTING A PERSON TO ONE'S CONTROL (YOUR HUSBAND).

(1 Peter 3:3-6, KJV)

[3] Whose adorning let it not be that outward adorning of plaiting the hair, and of wearing of gold, or of putting on of apparel;

[4] But **let it be the hidden man of the heart, in that which is not corruptible, even the ornament of a meek and quiet spirit, which is in the sight of God of great price.**

⁵ For after this manner in the old time the holy women also, who trusted in God, adorned themselves, **being in subjection unto their own husbands**:

⁶ Even as Sara obeyed Abraham, calling him lord: whose daughters ye are, as long as ye do well, and are not afraid with any amazement.

Do not let your adorning be external. Do not be so beautiful on the outside and a raving monster on the inside. No man wants to live with a beauty queen that is spoiled, self-centered, selfish, and wants her way all the time, ungrateful for what he does for her, can not be satisfied with anything, lazy, fighting, physically and verbally, fussing, and complaining all the time.

(1 Timothy 2:1-15, KJV)

First of all, then, I urge that supplications, prayers, intercessions, and thanksgivings be made for all people, for kings and all who are in high positions, that we may lead a peaceful and quiet life, godly and dignified in every way. This is good and it is **pleasing in the sight of God our Savior,** who desires all people to be saved and to come to the knowledge of the truth. For there is one God, and there is one mediator between God and men, the man Christ Jesus, ...

As a woman married to a Man of God you must make supplications, prayers, and intercession for your husband. Remember to pray for your husband because he is holding a high position in the House of the Lord. You must fast and pray to lead a peaceful and quiet life in your home with your husband and children. It's imperative to be godly and show a composed, serious manner that is worthy of respect by your husband and everyone.

(James 4:7, KJV)

Submit yourselves therefore to God. Resist the devil, and he will flee from you.

Holy women, when you have submitted yourself fully to God, you will automatically submit yourself to your husband. The devil does not want you to submit to your husband because he is against everything in God's word. Resist the devil and obey your husband. Be the best, sweet wife you can be. Resist the enemy by fasting, praying, and reading the Word. You have a weapon against satan, which is the Holy Bible. When you resist the devil, he can not stand the Word of God and he will flee from you.

(Titus 2:4-5, KJV)

[3] The **aged women** likewise, that they be in behaviour as becometh holiness, not false accusers, not given to much wine, **teachers of good things;**

[4] That they may **teach the young women** to be sober, to **love their husbands**, to **love their children,**

[5] To be discreet, chaste, keepers at home, good, **obedient to their own husbands**, that the word of God be not blasphemed.

I am an aged woman and I am currently sixty-six years old. I'm filled with the Holy Ghost, and have lived a Holy Life before God, my husband, my daughter, and the world. I fulfilled the life as a devoted minister's wife, Pastor's wife, Bishop's wife, and currently a Presiding Bishop wife and God told me to teach good things: To instruct and counsel the young women to love their husbands and children, to be self-controlled, pure, working at home if possible, kind, and submissive to their own husbands, that the Word of God may not be blasphemed.

Summary of **Wife Submit to Your Husband:**

When God keeps repeating in one chapter or in different chapters and scriptures about something **it is very, very important to Him** and He wants you to obey it. Look at all the scriptures in the new and old testament of the Bible stating that a woman is to <u>submit to her husband.</u>

1. **(Genesis 3:16, KJV):** thy desire shall be to thy husband, and he shall rule over thee.
2. **(Ephesians 5:21, KJV):** Submitting to one another out of reverence for Christ.
3. **(Ephesians 5:22, KJV):** Wives, submit to your own husbands, as to the Lord.
4. **(Ephesians 5:24, KJV):** Now as the church submits to Christ, so also wives should submit in everything to their husbands.
5. **(Colossians 3:18, KJV):** Wives, submit to your husbands, as is fitting in the Lord.
6. **(Titus 2:5, KJV):** To be self-controlled, pure, working at home, kind, and submissive to their own husbands, that the word of God may not be reviled.
7. **(1 Corinthians 11:3, KJV):** But I want you to understand that the head of every man is Christ, the head of a wife is her husband, and the head of Christ is God.
8. **(1 Peter 2:13, KJV):** Submit yourselves to every ordinance of man for the Lord's sake: whether it be to the king, as supreme;
9. **(1 Peter 3:1-2, KJV):** Likewise, ye wives, be in subjection to your own husbands; that, if any obey not the word, they

also may without the word be won by the conversation of the wives.

10. (**Colossians 3:18, KJV**): Wives, submit yourselves unto your own husbands, as it is fit in the Lord.

11. (**Titus 2:5, KJV**): To be discreet chaste, keepers at home, good, obedient to their own husbands, that the word of God be not blasphemed.

12. (**1 Peter 2:13, KJV**): Submit yourselves to every ordinance of man for the Lord's sake. Your husband.

13. (**1 Peter 3:1, KJV**): Likewise, ye wives, be in subjection to your own husbands;

14. (**1 Peter 3:5, KJV**): being in subjection unto their own husbands.

15. (**James 4:7, KJV**): Submit yourselves therefore to God. Resist the devil, and he will flee from you.

16. (**Titus 2:5, KJV**): obedient to their own husbands.

Love,
Elect Lady Judith A. Harrell
MAY GOD BLESS YOU.

Married into the ministry since 1975

I AM HIGHLY FAVORED BY GOD BECAUSE THE LORD ALLOWED ME TO SEEK FIRST THE KINGDOM OF GOD AND I MET THE MOST INCREDIBLE HUSBAND ON THE PLANET EARTH.

This is a book you do not want to miss. This book will answer most of your questions and heal you as

Someone married, but definitely if you're married to a man in the ministry.

ABOUT THE AUTHOR

Elect Lady Judith A. Harrell is an Assistant Pastor of Greater House of Faith Church in Virginia Beach, Va, where her husband is the founder, Pastor, and Bishop for forty-six years (46). She is also the Elect Lady of her husband's organization United International Pentecostal Assemblies (UIPA). He is the Presiding Bishop. She's been living with her husband (Bishop John S. Harrell) for forty-seven happy years. Their daughter (Shekinah Harrell) lives in San Diego, California. She is such a help, blessing to us, and still virtually active in our church and helps us in the ministry tremendously.

Printed in the United States
by Baker & Taylor Publisher Services